Table of Contents

Introduction

Types of Stories
- biographies
- other cultures
- life science
- physical science
- arts and crafts
- sports

Ways to Use the Stories
1. Directed lessons
   - with small groups of students reading at the same level
   - with an individual student

2. Partner reading

3. With cooperative learning groups

4. Independent practice
   - at school
   - at home

Things to Consider
1. Determine your purpose for selecting a story—instructional device, partner reading, group work, or independent reading. Each purpose calls for a different degree of story difficulty.

2. A single story may be used for more than one purpose. You might first use the story as an instructional tool, have partners read the story a second time for greater fluency, and then use the story at a later time for independent reading.

3. When presenting a story to a group or an individual for the first time, review any vocabulary that will be difficult to decode or understand. Many students will benefit from a review of the vocabulary page and the questions before they read the story.

Types of Skill Pages

Four pages of activities covering a wide variety of reading skills follow each story:

- comprehension
- vocabulary
- organizing information
- structural analysis
- parts of speech

Ways to Use the Skill Pages

1. Individualize skill practice for each student with tasks that are appropriate for his or her needs.

2. As directed minilessons, the skill pages may be used in several ways:

   - Make a transparency for students to follow as you work through the lesson.

   - Write the activity on the board and call on students to fill in the answers.

   - Reproduce the page for everyone to use as you direct the lesson.

3. When using the skill pages for independent practice, make sure that the skills have been introduced to the reader. Review the directions and check for understanding. Review the completed lesson with the student to determine if further practice is needed.

Tasmanian Devils

The Tasmanian devil has strong forelegs with five toes on each paw. The weaker hind paws have four toes. Bumpy pads on their paws help them climb trees.

After the sun sets in Tasmania, the night animals wake up. They don't have to set their alarm clocks. The screams of the Tasmanian devils tell them it's time to eat. When the nocturnal animals leave their daytime hideaways, they try to stay away from these unpleasant neighbors.

Tasmanian devils are always hungry. They can make a meal out of almost anything. If there is something to eat nearby, they'll find it. Their eyes see well at night, and they are talented food sniffers.

These scavengers are one of nature's important garbage collectors. Their favorite food is rotten meat. They feed on dead birds and animals. Their sharp teeth crush the toughest foods. They even swallow bones. The poisons and germs they eat don't seem to bother them. Their eating habits stop bacteria and disease from spreading to other animals. They keep the earth clean.

Tasmanian devils don't worry about good table manners. They scream with their mouths full. Chewing isn't in style. These carnivorous animals gulp down chunks of meat as fast as they can. They don't share, and they can eat ten times their weight in food at each meal.

Tasmanian devils have head-to-toe tempers. Their ears turn red when they are angry. They stomp their feet and turn from side to side to show off their teeth. That's not all. They scream and click their teeth too. If their tantrums don't scare enemies away, they give off smelly fluids from both ends of their bodies.

What happens when two Tasmanian devils meet? At first they try to scare off each other. If one decides not to fight, there are two ways to escape. One animal can let the other animal take a victory bite, or it can sprawl out on the ground on its belly. If neither animal gives up, they fight until one dies.

Tasmanian devils are black or brown with white patches or stripes. They aren't much bigger than a house cat when they are full-grown. Like the kangaroo, they are marsupials. The mother has a pouch for the babies.

Tasmanian devils are very tiny when they are born. After birth the $\frac{1}{4}$-inch-long (.6 centimeter) babies have to find their way to the mother's pouch. Mom feeds only the first four who climb into the pouch.

Like other mammals, the babies drink their mother's milk. They stay in the pouch for three months. The mother opens her pouch to clean the babies. When the babies have grown a few inches, they move to a nest of grass and leaves. They still take milk from the mother. After another three months, it's time to explore the world. They hang on to Mom's fur coat, and she takes them along to hunt for food.

When they are old enough to be on their own, the young leave home quickly. Like all Tasmanian devils, Mom has a bad temper and a big appetite. When she's hungry, she'll eat anything! That's one reason Tasmanian devils live by themselves in holes, hollow logs, and caves. ■

Name _____

Questions about *Tasmanian Devils*

1. When do Tasmanian devils look for food?

   _____

   _____

2. What is the function of the bumpy pads on a Tasmanian devil's paws?

   _____

   _____

3. In what ways are Tasmanian devils useful?

   _____

   _____

   _____

4. Tell six ways that Tasmanian devils show they are angry.

   _____

   _____

   _____

   _____

   _____

5. Using your own words, describe the traits of the Tasmanian devil.

   _____

   _____

   _____

6. Use a globe or an atlas to find the island of Tasmania, the home of the Tasmanian devils. This island is part of the country that lies to the north. What is the name of this country?

   _____

Tasmanian Devils
Think about It

1. Tasmanian devils used to live on the continent of Australia too. The farmers and ranchers didn't like them. They hunted and trapped these animals until there weren't any more of them. Write your opinion to answer the following two questions.

   a. Why do you think the ranchers and farmers didn't like the Tasmanian devils?

   _____

   _____

   b. Why do you think the people in Tasmania stopped hunting and trapping all the Tasmanian devils?

   _____

   _____

2. Tasmanian devils are solitary animals—they live by themselves. How does this help them survive?

   _____

   _____

3. Name another species (kind) of solitary animal.

   _____

   _____

4. Name two species of animals that live in family groups.

   _____

   _____

Name _____

Tasmanian Devils
Vocabulary

The words in the word box describe Tasmanian devils. Match these words with their definitions to fill in the spaces in the crossword puzzle.

Word Box

noisy
hungry
nocturnal
solitary
aggressive
mammals
smelly
marsupials
carnivorous
scavengers

The vertical word reads: TASMANIAN DEVILS

Across
1. animals that feed on dead matter
3. warm-blooded animals that drink milk from their mothers
4. active at night
5. meat-eating
7. having a bad odor
8. animals whose young are carried in the mother's pouch
9. alone, by itself

Down
2. quick to attack others
4. making loud sounds
6. needing food

Name _____

Tasmanian Devils
Categories

Next to each word listed below, write the names of two animals that the word describes.
Example: mammal—cats, horses

carnivorous   _____   _____

nocturnal   _____   _____

scavenger   _____   _____

marsupial   _____   _____

Compound Words

Complete each compound word found in the story. Then draw a line to its meaning.

them_____   a thing of any sort

_____time   a secret place

_____thing   close

hide_____   when there is sunlight

some_____   referring to them

_____by   once in a while

Japanese Celebrations

Children in Japan enjoy many festivals and special days throughout the year. Some of these festivals have been celebrated for hundreds of years, and many are just for children. Children also take part in activities during family and community holidays. Every month of the year in Japan, from New Year's Day through December, there are times to celebrate.

Children's Day

Children's Day, November 15th, is a festival that honors three-, five-, and seven-year-old children. On this day, the family visits a religious shrine to pray for the children's good health and happiness. The children are given bags of holiday candy. They are told that eating the candy will bring them good luck and a long life. The family celebrates the holiday with parties and presents for the children.

Boy's Day

Today, all children in Japan are honored on Boy's Day, but many traditions for this holiday are just for the boys in the family. On May 5th, at the beginning of the day, the family takes a special bath to wash away bad luck. Iris leaves are placed in the water to bring strength and bravery. A display with banners, toy weapons and armor, or figures of warriors wearing armor is set out for everyone to admire. Fathers often give their displays to their sons. Some of the weapons and the armor are very old. A brightly colored carp kite for each boy in the family is flown from a pole in front of the house. The oldest boy's kite is placed at the top of the pole, and his kite is the largest. The carp is a strong, courageous fish that swims upstream against the currents. It's hoped that the boys in the family will be strong and courageous like the carp.

Hina Matsuri

Hina Matsuri, the doll festival, is celebrated every year on the third day of the third month. On this day, girls display a special set of dolls called *hina* [hee' na]. Grandmothers and mothers often give their sets of dolls to the young daughters in the family. Many collections are very old and valuable. There are figures of the emperor and empress, ladies-in-waiting, the minister of state, court musicians, and courtiers, all dressed in traditional clothing. The older dolls have painted porcelain faces and glass eyes. Some of the newer dolls, however, are made of plastic.

The dolls are displayed on a tiered stand covered with a red cloth. Special furniture and replicas of food are placed with the dolls. Girls visit with each other and admire the doll collections. They share rice cakes and tea.

After the holiday, the dolls are carefully stored away for the following year.

The Gion Festival

In 869 in Kyoto, there was an epidemic and many people became ill. The emperor prayed to the gods for his people's health. He sent an offering of weapons to the Gion Shrine. When his prayers were answered and people were no longer suffering from the disease, the grateful emperor organized a big parade to celebrate the first Gion Festival.

Today, huge decorated boxes called *hokos* are paraded through the streets. Some of the boxes are hundreds of years old. They weigh many tons and can be as tall as a four-story building. The boxes are set on huge wheels about eight feet in diameter. After the parade the hokos are taken apart and carefully stored for the next festival.

Each year before the festival, a boy is selected for a special role. First he is dressed up like a priest and his face is painted white. Then he inspects the hokos while they are put back together. Someone walks with him and holds an umbrella over his head to shade him from the sun.

Right before the parade, the boy takes his place of honor on top of a hoko. There he has a bird's-eye view of the celebration while the hoko is pulled along the parade route.

Page Boy

Happy New Year

During the New Year celebration on January 1, everyone in the family celebrates a birthday. Each person is one year older on that day. It doesn't matter when the person's day of birth really is. A child born on May 2 and one born on October 10 will both celebrate their first birthday on January 1.

Greeting cards and family visits are other important traditions for the New Year. Girls play a game similar to badminton, and boys fly kites and spin tops. Children buy strips of paper with fortunes written on them and tie them like blossoms on bare winter trees. They hope this will bring them good luck in the new year.

Tanabata

During Tanabata, the Festival of the Stars, Japanese children put up a bamboo tree. They write poems and hang them from the tree. Schools, and even the family doorway, are decorated with poems.

The Sapporo Snow Festival

The whole family enjoys the Sapporo Snow Festival. During the winter months, people come to Sapporo in northern Japan to enjoy winter sports. On the second Thursday of each winter month, teams of artists carve enormous ice and snow sculptures. Some of the sculptures are more than 60 feet tall. ∎

Name _____

Questions about
Japanese Celebrations

1. Why do you think Boy's Day is no longer just for boys?

   _____

   _____

2. Why did the emperor organize a parade to celebrate the first Gion Festival?

   _____

   _____

3. When do people in Japan celebrate their birthdays?

   _____

4. Which Japanese festival would you like to attend? Why?

   _____

   _____

   _____

5. Write the letter of each activity next to the holiday where it belongs.

   a. Carp kites are flown.
   b. Huge decorated boxes are paraded through the streets.
   c. Special dolls are displayed.
   d. Everyone celebrates a birthday.
   e. Iris leaves are placed in the bath water.
   f. A boy dresses like a priest and inspects the hokos.
   g. Children write poems and hang them from bamboo trees.
   h. Special furniture and replicas of food are placed with the dolls.
   i. Children are given bags of candy.

   New Year _____   Gion Festival _____   Boy's Day _____

   Children's Day _____   Hina Matsuri _____   Tanabata _____

Name _____

Japanese Celebrations
Vocabulary

1. Write three words used in the story that mean "special day."

   _____

2. What are the titles of the dolls displayed on Hina Matsuri?

   _____

   _____

3. Where do families go to pray on Children's Day?

   _____

4. What is another word for the snow and ice figures carved for the Sapporo Snow Festival?

   _____

5. Write the letter of each word by its definition. Use the clues in the story to help you decide what the words mean.

   a. badminton   _____ very brave

   b. diameter   _____ the name of a species of fish

   c. carp   _____ a disease affecting a lot of people

   d. current   _____ customs that are repeated year after year

   e. collection   _____ persons who serve royalty

   f. epidemic   _____ very fancy, with great detail

   g. courtiers   _____ a game

   h. elaborate   _____ the flow of water in a stream or river

   i. traditions   _____ a group of objects

   j. courageous   _____ a straight line that passes through the center of circle

Name _____

Japanese Celebrations
Suffixes

Here are some words from the story that have endings or suffixes. Write the root word and the suffix. Be careful, because some words may have a spelling change.

Word	Root Word	Suffix
largest	large	est
celebration	_____	_____
happiness	_____	_____
beginning	_____	_____
brightly	_____	_____
courageous	_____	_____
collections	_____	_____
valuable	_____	_____
covered	_____	_____
carefully	_____	_____

Write two sentences using words from the list above. Use **two** words in each sentence.

1. _____

   _____

2. _____

   _____

Japanese Celebrations

Description

Find the words in the story that describe the things mentioned below.

1. _____ , _____ fish

2. _____ _____ carp kite

3. _____ _____ faces

4. _____ _____ boxes

5. _____ _____ trees

6. _____ _____ and _____ sculptures

Choose interesting adjectives of your own to describe the things below.

1. _____ _____ tower

2. _____ _____ meadow

3. _____ _____ car

4. _____ _____ sweater

5. _____ _____ vase

Good Earth Times

Hooray for Weeds!

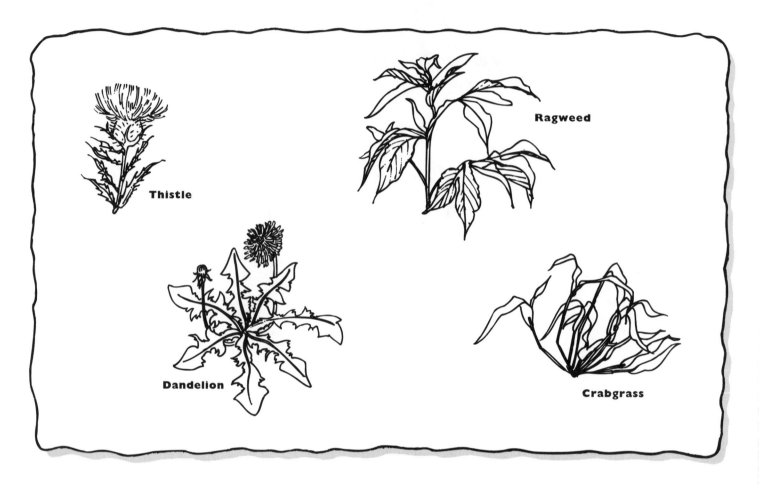

Weeds are the uninvited guests of the plant world. They sprout up in gardens, forests, meadows, and pastures. They put down their roots in places where other plants can't grow. Gardeners don't like to see weeds, but weeds are important in many ways.

Like other green plants, weeds capture the energy of the sun and turn it into food. Muskrats enjoy nutritious vitamins and minerals when they eat cattails. Gophers and mice chew the tasty roots of many weeds. Some weeds produce seeds or berries that are valuable food sources for insects, birds, and other animals. When they absorb water, roots pull in minerals and vitamins from the soil. Animals that eat the roots or other parts of weeds add needed minerals and vitamins to their diets.

Humans can enjoy eating some kinds of weeds too. Chickweed is not welcome in lawns and gardens, but it is a nutritious plant. Its leaves can be gathered and cooked like spinach.

Both man and beast can eat all parts of the common dandelion. The plant is rich in vitamins A and C, as well as important minerals. The yellow flowers can be picked before the buds open and then roasted. Tea can be made from the boiled roots. The leaves can be picked in the spring and boiled. The result is a green, leafy vegetable that tastes a little like spinach. Rodents feed on dandelion roots, bees gather pollen and nectar from the flowers, and horses eat the leaves.

Weeds can be a source of important calcium. When an animal dies, its bones deposit calcium in the soil. Weed roots absorb the calcium. The plant you eat today might contain calcium that was in the skull of a saber-toothed tiger! Decaying weeds put calcium back into the soil. When the soil is washed into a stream or an ocean, algae and other microscopic water plants absorb the calcium. Fish eat these plants. When people and animals eat these fish, they add needed calcium to their diets.

Weeds also help the soil. They loosen the soil with their roots so that it's easier for insects and animals to dig in the soil. When weeds die, bacteria and fungi in the soil break up the decaying weeds to form more soil.

The roots of weeds hold rich topsoil in place so that it doesn't wash away in heavy rains and wind. By holding the soil in place and preventing erosion, weeds keep streams and rivers from clogging with mud and chemicals. Fish and animals in the rivers and streams die when they don't have clean water.

If the streams are choked with sediment, they can flood fields and cause damage to food crops. Hydroelectric power plants can't operate if the rivers are filled with sediment.

But the benefits of the humble weed don't stop here. A patch of prickly weeds like the wild rose can shelter rabbits, birds, and other small animals. Hawks and large predators can't get through the maze of stickers to find their prey. Giant weeds act as shields and slow strong winds. When fires destroy forests and grassland, rain and wind blow away the good topsoil. If enough fast-growing weeds sprout up, they will hold the soil in place during winter storms.

Weeds are an important part of the plant and animal kingdom. The world is a better place to live because of their work. The next time you see a dandelion, cattail, poison ivy, or soapweed plant, say thanks for a job well done.

Weeds provide food for wild animals. Here, a vole nibbles on dandelion roots.

Read and Understand, Nonfiction • Grades 4–6 • EMC 749

Name _____

Questions about *Hooray for Weeds!*

A. Write these words in the blanks to complete the sentences.

tea	chickweed	nutritious	topsoil	vitamins
prickly	dandelion	fires	minerals	calcium

1. Weeds absorb nutritious _____ and _____ from the soil.

2. Many animals that eat weeds are healthier because weeds are _____.

3. Decaying weeds put _____ back into the soil.

4. Weeds help hold _____ in place.

5. _____ can be made from the roots of the _____ plant.

6. Both dandelion and _____ leaves taste a bit like spinach.

7. _____ weeds serve as shelter for small animals.

8. Fast-growing weeds can hold the soil in place after forest _____.

B. Answer these questions.

1. What are two ways in which weeds help fish?

_____

_____

2. Why do you think gardeners don't appreciate the benefits of weeds?

_____

_____

3. How do weeds prevent wind and rain from eroding topsoil?

_____

_____

Hooray for Weeds!

Fact and Opinion

Facts are statements that are true. **Opinions** are ideas or feelings that people believe.

1. Here is an opinion given in the story:

   Weeds are an important part of the plant and animal kingdom. The world is a better place to live because of their work.

   Many facts in the story support the opinion by showing ways in which weeds are important.

   List 10 facts that tell ways in which weeds help plants, animals, people, and the earth.

   _____

   _____

   _____

   _____

   _____

   _____

   _____

   _____

   _____

   _____

   _____

2. The story says that gardeners don't like to see weeds. Write an opinion that a gardener might have about uninvited weeds in his or her garden. Then write a fact about weeds that would support this opinion.

   _____

   _____

   _____

Name _____

Hooray For Weeds!
Vocabulary

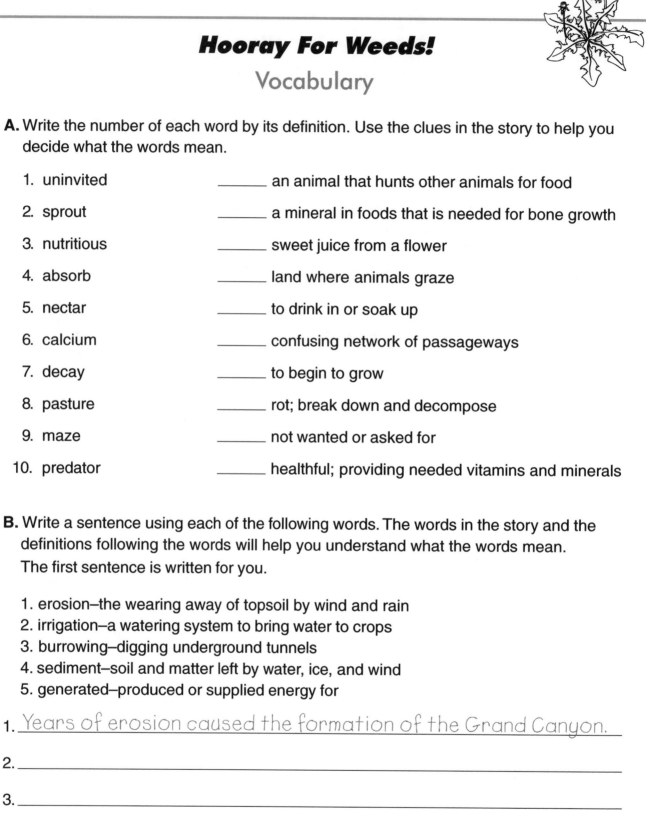

A. Write the number of each word by its definition. Use the clues in the story to help you decide what the words mean.

1. uninvited	_____ an animal that hunts other animals for food
2. sprout	_____ a mineral in foods that is needed for bone growth
3. nutritious	_____ sweet juice from a flower
4. absorb	_____ land where animals graze
5. nectar	_____ to drink in or soak up
6. calcium	_____ confusing network of passageways
7. decay	_____ to begin to grow
8. pasture	_____ rot; break down and decompose
9. maze	_____ not wanted or asked for
10. predator	_____ healthful; providing needed vitamins and minerals

B. Write a sentence using each of the following words. The words in the story and the definitions following the words will help you understand what the words mean. The first sentence is written for you.

1. erosion—the wearing away of topsoil by wind and rain
2. irrigation—a watering system to bring water to crops
3. burrowing—digging underground tunnels
4. sediment—soil and matter left by water, ice, and wind
5. generated—produced or supplied energy for

1. _Years of erosion caused the formation of the Grand Canyon._

2. _____

3. _____

4. _____

5. _____

Name _____

Hooray for Weeds!

Synonyms and Antonyms

Synonyms are words that have the same or nearly the same meaning.
Antonyms are words that have opposite meanings.

A. Read the pairs of words below.
   If the words are synonyms, write **S** on the line.
   If the words are antonyms, write **A** on the line.

decay	rot	_____	stream	river	_____
predator	prey	_____	soil	earth	_____
absorb	soak up	_____	benefit	harm	_____
healthy	nutritious	_____	shelter	protect	_____
uninvited	welcome	_____	destroy	ruin	_____
valuable	worthless	_____	prickly	smooth	_____

B. Write pairs of antonyms to complete the sentences.

1. I had felt _____ after a good night's sleep, but the 10-mile run left me

   feeling _____.

2. After the deep _____ of the cave, the sudden _____ of the

   screeching birds startled us.

3. We like our home and want to _____ there, but Dad has a new job

   and we must _____ to a new city.

4. You'd think that twins would be the _____, but Joe and Harry are very

   _____ from each other.

Marian Anderson

Marian Anderson was the first African American to sing a major role at the Metropolitan Opera House in New York City. She began her singing career when she joined the junior choir at her church at the age of six. After a few years, she was singing in both the junior and senior choirs. Visitors who came to the church enjoyed Marian's singing. They often invited her and the choir to sing in other churches or for special community occasions. Marian's parents knew she had a special gift for music, but they couldn't afford to pay for lessons.

Her father died when she was young, and Marian, her sister, and her mother moved to her grandparents' house. Marian's mother worked

Marian Anderson, 1897–1993

hard cleaning houses and washing clothes to support the girls. At first, when Marian earned money by singing, she gave the money to her mother. Later she was able to use some of the money for music lessons.

Music was Anderson's favorite subject in school. When she was in high school, she joined the Philadelphia Choral Society. Because she was becoming well known, she often sang in other cities. She had to miss classes at school when she was out of town, but her teachers helped her make up her work.

Anderson knew she would have to study music and take singing lessons if she wanted to keep singing. A voice teacher agreed to give her music lessons without charge. With the teacher's help, Anderson learned new ways to control her voice when she sang.

While Marian was growing up, many public facilities were segregated. When Marian was invited to Georgia to sing, she and her mother had to ride in the section of the train that was set aside for African Americans. They weren't allowed to eat in the dining car. When Marian sang in New York and other cities, she had to stay in hotels for African Americans. These hotels were often far from the places where she was singing.

Many businesses and schools discriminated against African Americans. Anderson wanted to enroll in a Philadelphia music school after high school so she could learn more about music. When she went to the school for an application, she was told she couldn't attend the school because she was African American.

But Marian didn't give up the idea of a singing career because she couldn't attend the music school. She continued to take private lessons with voice teachers. Her church raised money so she could study with a famous teacher. He helped her improve her singing, and she began to earn more money from her concerts. She won a competition to sing with the New York Philharmonic Orchestra. Marian worked hard to learn foreign languages so she could sing songs written in other languages. She went to Europe to study music and languages. She was invited to sing in Norway, Sweden, and Finland. Many famous European composers and musicians came to her successful concerts. On her second trip to Europe, she stayed for two years and sang in many different countries.

Even though Marian had become famous, she was still not allowed to stay in some hotels or eat in many restaurants in the United States. Once Marian was scheduled to sing in Constitution Hall in Washington, D.C., the nation's capital, but the concert was canceled because African Americans were not allowed to perform there. Other auditoriums refused to allow her to sing too.

Many people were angry to learn that one of this country's greatest singers couldn't sing in the nation's capital. Finally, the government of the United States invited Anderson to sing on the steps of the Lincoln Memorial in Washington, D.C., on Easter Sunday. More than 75,000 people, black and white, sat together and listened to her concert. Later in her career, Anderson sang at the White House.

In 1955 Anderson became the first African-American artist to have a major operatic role at the Metropolitan Opera House in New York City. After her Metropolitan success, she performed in many more countries around the world. Her voice and her courage were admired everywhere.

The United States government sent Anderson to sing and meet people all over the world. She was appointed to be a member of the American delegation to the United Nations. She retired from her singing career in 1965. Up until her death in 1993, Marian Anderson continued to receive recognition for her music and for her work with people all over the world.

Questions about
Marian Anderson

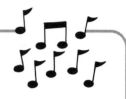

1. Why do you think a voice teacher agreed to give Marian lessons without charge?

   _____

2. Why wasn't Marian allowed to fill out an application for a music school?

   _____

3. Why was it difficult for Marian to sing away from home in the United States?

   _____

   _____

4. Why did Anderson take her first trip to Europe?

   _____

   _____

5. Why was Anderson's concert at Constitution Hall canceled?

   _____

6. Why was Anderson's performance in an opera at the Metropolitan Opera House in New York City important?

   _____

7. Do you agree or disagree with the following statement?

   Marian Anderson was a very brave person.

   Give details from the story to support your opinion.

   _____

   _____

   _____

   _____

Name _____

Marian Anderson

In the biography about Marian Anderson, the events are in chronological order except for the first sentence. **Chronological order** means the events are listed in the order in which they happened.

1. Number the events in Marian Anderson's life in chronological order. Number each set separately. You may need to reread parts of the story.

Set A

_____ Marian's father died.

_____ She sang in both the junior and senior choirs.

_____ She began her career when she was six years old.

_____ Marian Anderson was born in 1897.

Set B

_____ She gave concerts in Norway, Sweden, and Finland

_____ Her church raised money so she could study with a famous voice teacher.

_____ Marian didn't give up the idea of a singing career because she couldn't attend music school.

_____ Anderson went to Europe to study music and languages.

Set C

_____ Marian was appointed to be a member of the American delegation to the United Nations.

_____ Anderson's concert at Constitution Hall was canceled.

_____ Anderson retired from her singing career in 1965.

_____ Anderson was the first African American to sing a major role at the Metropolitan Opera House in New York City.

2. Select three events in Marian Anderson's singing career that you think were important. Write them in chronological order on the lines below.

_____

_____

_____

_____

Marian Anderson

Vocabulary

Choose the best word to complete each sentence.

retired   appointed   career   discriminated   enroll   foreign
composer   competition   recognition   segregated   application   languages

1. To apply for a school or a job, you need to fill out an _____.

2. If you want to study to be a doctor, you must _____ in a
medical school.

3. Marian Anderson wanted to study singing so that she could have a musical

_____.

4. Marian traveled to many _____ countries to perform
concerts.

5. When Anderson was 68, she _____ from her singing
career.

6. An opera singer must sing songs in many _____.

7. Marian received _____ for her music.

8. Anderson was _____ to be a member of the American
delegation to the United Nations.

9. When Marian was singing in the United States, many hotels and restaurants

were _____.

10. Even though Constitution Hall in Washington, D.C., _____
against African-American performers, Anderson was able to sing a concert in
the nation's capital.

11. Marian won a _____ to sing with the New York Philharmonic
Orchestra.

12. A _____ is a person who writes music.

Marian Anderson
Suffixes

1. When the suffix **tion** is added to a word, the word becomes a noun. Each of the following verbs has a noun form in the story that ends with **tion**. Find the noun and write it next to the verb.

   a. apply _____

   b. compete _____

   c. recognize _____

2. Write a sentence using one of the verb forms above.

   _____

   _____

3. Here are two nouns that end with **tion**. In the story you will find another form of these words. Find the words and write them on the lines.

   Noun Form

   a. discrimina**tion** _____

   b. segrega**tion** _____

4. The following verbs are found in the story. Add the suffix **ment** to change the verbs to nouns. Write the new words next to the verbs. (Hint: You may have to take off an ending first.)

Verb Form	Noun Form
a. retired	_____
b. appointed	_____
c. enroll	_____

5. Write a sentence using one of the **ment** words you wrote.

   _____

   _____

©1999 by Evan-Moor Corp.   27   Read and Understand, Nonfiction • Grades 4–6 • EMC 749

Gold, Gold, Gold!

Bend it, twist it, pound it, or roll it out! Gold is the softest metal and the easiest one to shape. A thin wire, 62 miles (99.8 kilometers) long, can be formed from 1.02 ounces (28.9 grams) of gold. Gold can be pressed into sheets that are as thin as a piece of paper.

Even though gold can be molded into different shapes, it doesn't dissolve or change when it's in water or in most other liquids. It doesn't melt until it reaches $1,947\frac{1}{4}°$ F, and it boils only when it reaches a very hot $2,808\frac{1}{4}°$ F

Specks and small pieces of gold are found in river and stream beds. Prospectors separate the gold from the gravel. The simplest way to do this is to pan the gold. Gravel is scooped up in a circular dish. The prospector swirls it around and washes it with water. The lighter gravel washes away, leaving the gold behind. Sluice boxes and machines are also used to separate gold and gravel.

Gold is also found in the oceans. There are nine billion metric tons of it in the world's salty seas. It costs more money to mine the gold out of the sea than the gold is worth. For that reason, it will stay in the oceans until someone finds new, inexpensive ways to collect it.

Large deposits of gold are under the ground. Deposits of silver are often found with the gold. One of the biggest gold nuggets ever discovered is named Welcome Stranger. It weighs about 156 pounds (71 kilograms). It didn't come from a mine. It was found on the ground near Victoria, Australia, in 1869.

Even though gold is found in many places around the world, it is rare. There isn't very much of it. Today, more gold is mined in South Africa than in any other country. It supplies about 6,000,000 metric tons every year. South Africa, the United States, the former Soviet Republics, Australia, Canada, China, and Brazil produce most of the world's gold.

From 1934 to 1975, it was illegal for a person in the United States to own large amounts of gold. Only small objects and jewelry made from this precious metal were allowed. Even though people can own gold today, not many people carry it in their pockets in place of money. It's very heavy. One cubic inch of gold weighs about a pound (0.45 kilogram).

Gold has many uses. Long ago many coins were pressed from gold. For thousands of years, people have worn gold jewelry. Gold labeled 24 karat is pure gold. Because this is too soft, most gold for jewelry is mixed with other metals. Some jewelry sold today has a gold coating or a wash that covers a harder metal. In the United States, gold school rings are one of the most popular kinds of jewelry.

Gold can be used in electronic parts because heat or water doesn't ruin it. It conducts electricity very well. Circuit boards and very small chips can be made with gold.

Gold reflects sunlight. The *Apollo* spacecraft was coated with gold to protect it from solar heat. The astronauts had a film of gold over their faceplates so the sun wouldn't injure their eyes. The windows on office buildings can be covered with see-through sheets of gold that help keep the building cool.

Many decorations are made with gold. Signs with gold letters are seen on office doors and windows. Gold letters can also be found in books.

Gold is used in some medical treatments for cancer, arthritis, and eye surgery. Gold is very useful because it doesn't change its form the way many other metals do when mixed with body fluids. Dentists used to make fillings for teeth from gold. Because gold is valuable, older gold fillings are often replaced, and the gold is recycled. ■

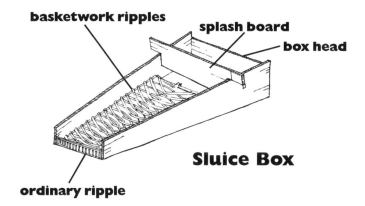

Sluice Box

basketwork ripples

splash board

box head

ordinary ripple

Questions about
Gold, Gold, Gold!

1. Name three reasons why gold is used in so many different ways.

_____

_____

_____

2. Why don't people mine the gold that is in the ocean?

_____

3. Name two ways gold has been used in the space program.

_____

_____

4. Would you buy jewelry that is labeled 24-karat gold? Why or why not?

_____

_____

5. What country produces more gold each year than any other?

_____

6. Describe how people pan for gold.

_____

_____

_____

_____

Name _____

Gold, Gold, Gold!

Think about It

1. If someone says, "You are worth your weight in gold," what does he or she really mean?

_____

_____

2. Proverbs are phrases or sentences that give advice. The proverb "a stitch in time saves nine" means that if you fix small problems, they won't turn into big ones. For example, if you pick up your room every day, it will stay neat. If you don't pick it up every day, by the end of the week it will be messy and take much longer to clean.

   Think about the proverb "All that glitters isn't gold." What do you think this proverb means?

_____

_____

_____

3. Why is gold so valuable?

_____

_____

4. Name some famous stories that show how valuable gold is.

_____

_____

_____

Bonus:
If gold sells for $250.00 an ounce, how much would you be worth if you were made of gold?

_____

Name _____

Gold, Gold, Gold!

Homophones

Words that sound the same but have different meanings are called **homophones**.

A. Find a homophone for each of the following words in the story, *Gold, Gold, Gold!*
Write the homophone and its definition as used in the story.

1. role–the part an actor has in a play

_____

2. peace–calm

_____

3. sea–a large salty body of water

_____

4. knew–had knowledge

_____

5. knot–looping of a cord

_____

6. carrot–a root vegetable

_____

7. sew–stitch with needle and thread

_____

B. *Mine* is a homophone with more than one meaning. It means "ownership; something that belongs to me." It also means "an underground hole where people search for gold, coal, or precious metals." Write a sentence using the words *gold mine.* Write another sentence using the word *mine* to show ownership.

1. _____

_____

2. _____

_____

Name _____

Gold, Gold, Gold!
Find the Good Luck Mine

Melissa found directions to the Good Luck Mine. She decided that a map would be easier to follow. Follow the directions to help Melissa draw the map in the box below, starting at the **X**.

• Use a ruler to draw the lines. Use this scale:

$\frac{1}{2}$ inch = $\frac{1}{4}$ mile   1 inch = $\frac{1}{2}$ mile   2 inches = 1 mile

• At each landmark, mark a • and also label the landmark.

Walk $\frac{1}{4}$ mile north from the old oak tree to Rocky Peak. Turn west. Continue one mile to Stony Ridge. Turn south. Walk one mile to Boulder Creek. Turn to the east and walk one mile to Pebble Road. Travel $\frac{1}{2}$ mile north to Gravel Gulch. Turn to the west. Walk $\frac{1}{2}$ mile to Granite Mountain. You'll see the entrance to the Good Luck Mine.

Now underline all the words for rocks that are in the directions. Circle two words that mean "small rocks."

Bonus:

On another paper, write a story about what you found when you explored the mine.

The Ants Go Marching

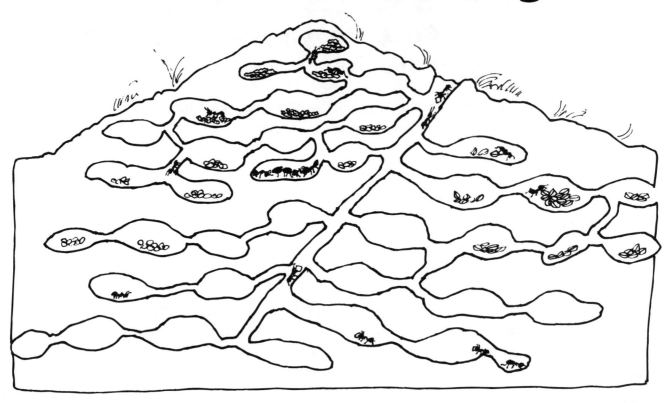

Ants can be found in most parts of the world. They build many kinds of homes. Some ant houses are made from paper, others are in trees, and many are under the ground. Ants tunnel through the ground, digging out subterranean rooms for their cities. They move the earth one grain at a time. Some homes are as deep as a one-story house. Often ant homes are solar heated. The tunnels are under a rock that is warmed by the sun. The rooms under that rock stay warm and dry.

Some ants build mound structures as tall as five feet or even higher. To build these houses, ants dig grains of wet soil from the ground and carry them to the mound. Sometimes they pack mud around blades of grass to make the walls stronger. They may bring pine needles to the mound to make the roof.

Carpenter ants tunnel into wood in fence posts, tree stumps, and even houses to make their homes. Some ants that don't like to build houses make their homes in bamboo or other hollow plants.

In South American rainforests, ants carry mud from the ground to a tree branch. The mud is packed around the branch and living quarters are tunneled into the mud ball. The ants gather seeds and plant them inside the mud. Roots sprout and twist around inside the ball, making it strong so heavy rains won't wash it away. The mud ball blooms, and the ants enjoy the food from their hanging gardens.

One kind of ant chews leaves, wood, and flowers to make paper houses. Their saliva and the plants form a paste. The ants shape the paste into a house and let it dry.

Harvester ants clear weeds and grass around their houses to make "roads." That way they can quickly bring home the food they gather.

All the ants in a community have special jobs. Some care for the larvae and young. They clean and feed the queen, who lays all the eggs. Other ant workers are herders who take care of aphids. They shelter them in the winter and take them to the plants when the weather is warmer. They milk the aphids by stroking the sides of these tiny insects. The aphids give off a sticky sap that is licked up by the ants. The ants carry the juice back to their homes where it is stored for later use or fed to the other ants. A very special group of ants guard the home and let only the ants that live there enter. They watch out for ants that try to kidnap larvae to raise them to be slaves.

Some ants are farmers. They carve enormous cities under the ground in which to farm fungi. Leaf cutters carry chunks of leaves back to their home. Chewers grind the leaves into a yellow paste. Other ants spread the paste inside the underground rooms. This paste fertilizes and helps fungi grow. The ants care for their crops and keep the food supply growing.

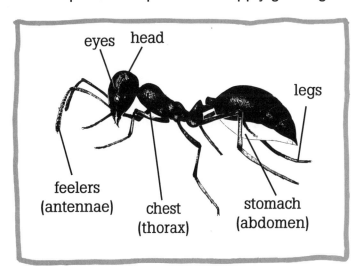

Even though we don't welcome the columns of ants that march into our kitchens looking for food, we can admire the way they work together to help their communities. They are amazing insects. ■

Name _____

Questions about
The Ants Go Marching

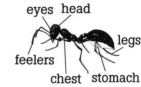

1. Why is it dangerous to have carpenter ants in your house?

_____

2. Where would you go to see ants building hanging garden houses?

_____

3. What do the ants grow in their underground farms?

_____

4. How do ants care for their herds of aphids?

_____

_____

5. In winter, when it is very cold, some ant communities crowd together in a ball. They keep changing places from the inside to the outside of the ball. How does this help the ants?

_____

_____

6. Write the letter of each thing that ants do on the line in front its effect.

   a. Harvester ants build roads   _____ to get a sticky sap.

   b. Because carpenter ants eat through wood,   _____ to make mounds stronger.

   c. Ants rub aphids   _____ they are not liked by people.

   d. Leaf paste is spread on walls   _____ to gather food faster.

   e. Mud is packed around blades of grass   _____ to fertilize fungi.

Name _____

The Ants Go Marching

Synonyms

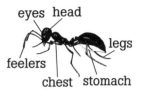

eyes head
legs
feelers
chest stomach

Synonyms are words that mean almost the same thing. Use a dictionary to help you understand the meanings of the following words. Then find the words in the story that have almost the same meanings.

1. types   _____

2. subterranean   _____

3. excavate   _____

4. active   _____

5. collect   _____

6. gigantic   _____

7. construct   _____

8. protects   _____

Irregular Plurals

Most plural forms are made by adding **s** or **es**. The words listed below form plurals in a different way.

Read the singular nouns below. Find the plural forms in the story.

1. fungus   _____

2. larva   _____

3. leaf   _____

4. city   _____

Name _____

The Ants Go Marching

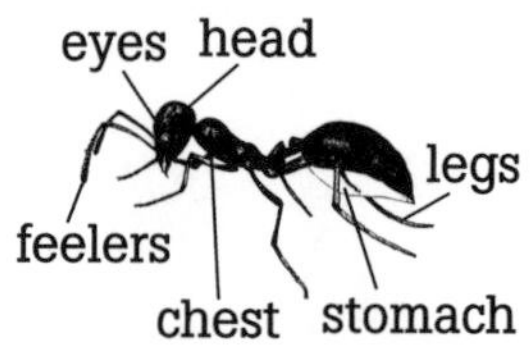

eyes head
legs
feelers
chest stomach

Draw a picture to show different ways ants build houses.
Show at least three types of ant homes.

Name _____

The Ants Go Marching

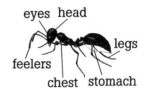

eyes head
legs
feelers
chest stomach

Alphabetical Order

Write these words from the story in alphabetical order.
Then find and circle each word in the word search.

harvester	weeds	enormous	aphids	fungi	tunnels	subterranean	saliva
sprout	carpenter	mound	grains	hollow	larvae	columns	bamboo

_____

_____

_____

_____

_____

_____

_____

_____

_____

_____

_____

_____

```
R  M  O  U  N  D  Z  H  P  E  Z  Q  G
S  S  S  A  L  I  V  A  Q  K  S  C  R
U  A  Q  R  H  M  T  R  W  D  F  O  A
B  A  M  B  O  O  M  V  E  D  Z  L  I
T  V  A  D  L  T  Z  E  N  M  O  U  N
E  C  O  L  L  M  W  S  O  R  E  M  S
R  S  P  R  O  U  T  T  R  T  B  N  A
R  Y  U  Y  W  A  X  E  M  U  G  S  P
A  R  P  E  N  T  E  R  O  N  Q  U  H
N  A  T  S  E  A  M  F  U  N  G  I  I
E  D  Z  K  V  D  N  N  S  E  S  G  D
A  F  T  R  O  A  T  O  S  L  D  E  S
N  D  A  T  R  V  F  L  T  S  P  W  M
K  L  C  A  R  P  E  N  T  E  R  C  D
```

Picturing History: The Story of Matthew Brady and His Camera

Matthew Brady was fascinated with the new camera portraits of people that were being taken in France in the late 1830s. These pictures were called daguerreotypes (də ger · ə tīps). While he worked at other jobs, Brady studied chemistry and learned everything he could from people who knew how to take these pictures.

Up to that time, people had to hire artists to paint their pictures. Often, the artist improved the way a person looked so he would receive more money for the portrait. Pictures made with a camera were more accurate.

In 1844 Brady opened a photographic studio in New York City and began to use this new photography process. It was very difficult to make a daguerreotype. First, Brady prepared a box with a silver surface and exposed it to iodine vapors. Next, he placed the silver box inside another box. In 5 to 30 minutes, the surface, or plate, turned yellow. The box had to be placed in the camera at just the right time. The person being photographed had to sit without moving for up to 30 minutes. If the picture turned out too light or too dark, it had to be taken again.

Matthew Brady, 1823–1896

There was no way to tell what the photograph would look like until the yellow plate was in the darkroom. There, under dim candlelight, the plate was placed in a box and exposed to heated mercury. When the image appeared, it was fixed with a solution of salt. These pictures were very delicate. Even rubbing with a soft cloth could rub away the picture. The picture was protected in a glass-covered box. Gradually, with better chemicals and methods, people didn't have to sit so long. A photograph could be taken in 15 seconds.

Many famous people came to Brady for their pictures. His studios photographed all the presidents from John Quincy Adams to William McKinley. A portrait of Abraham Lincoln is one of Brady's most well-known pictures. Singers, people in the theater, and famous writers came to Brady to have their portraits taken. King Edward VII of England took time for a portrait at Brady's when he stopped in New York on his way to Canada.

Matthew opened a second gallery in Washington, D.C., and began photographing famous people in the nation's capital. As his two studios expanded, he had to hire assistants to help with the work. More assistants were needed as Matthew's eyesight, always poor, grew worse.

In 1851 Matthew took 45 daguerreotypes to the World's Fair in England. He won a silver medal for his collection. In the United States he won more prizes for his work.

In 1860, when the American Civil War began, Brady thought it was important to take pictures to preserve the war for history. Because the pictures had to be developed right after they were taken, Brady carted his equipment, darkroom, and helpers to battlefields and army camps. During the Battle of Bull Run, his wagon was destroyed when the Union Army had to retreat. Brady made his way back to Washington, D.C., on foot.

Matthew continued to take photographs of the battles that took place near Washington, D.C. His pictures were put in books. At that time, people didn't want to be reminded about the war, and very few people bought the books.

Because Matthew spent so much time photographing the generals and the war, his studios began to lose money. To save his photography business, he tried to sell his collection of photographs to the government. In 1871 Congress agreed to buy 2,000 portraits, but they didn't set aside money for the purchase. Because Matthew could not pay his debts, sheriff's deputies came to take over his New York studio. Fortunately, he was able to take out many loads of photographs before the lawmen arrived.

The government finally gave Brady $25,000 for many of his pictures, and he was able to continue his work in Washington, D.C. He finished his presidential collection by photographing the presidents that were still living. In 1881 Brady closed his last studio.

The government did not take care of the plates they had purchased, so Matthew's collection was damaged and in need of restoration. When the government refused to pay to save his photographs, many priceless, historical pictures were ruined.

Today, when we see the copies of the Brady photos that survived, we know what Abraham Lincoln and many other famous people really looked like. We can see scenes from the Civil War because Matthew Brady, his camera, and his photographic assistants were there.

Questions about
The Story of Matthew Brady and His Camera

1. How did people get pictures of themselves before there were cameras?

_____

2. Why were the first daguerreotypes not well suited for taking pictures of people?

_____

_____

3. Why do you think famous people wanted to be photographed by Matthew Brady?

_____

_____

4. Why did Matthew decide to photograph the Civil War?

_____

_____

5. Why didn't people want to buy Brady's books with pictures of the Civil War?

_____

_____

6. Why were many of Brady's pictures ruined?

_____

_____

7. Why was Brady's work with the camera important?

_____

_____

The Story of Matthew Brady and His Camera

Sequence Steps and Events

A. Brady took the following steps to make a daguerreotype. Fill in the missing steps.

Before taking the picture:

1. Prepare a box with a silver surface.

2. _____

3. Place the silver box inside another box.

4. _____

5. Place the box in the camera.

After taking the picture:

6. Put the picture in a box.

7. _____

8. Fix the picture with a solution of salt.

9. _____

B. Six dates are given in the story. List each date and write a brief statement about the events that happened at that time.

_____ _____

_____ _____

_____ _____

_____ _____

_____ _____

The Story of Matthew Brady and His Camera

Vocabulary

A. Write each word below next to its definition.

accurate   vapors   adjustments   portrait   studio
gallery   retreat   engravings   priceless   daguerreotypes

1. gaseous forms of chemicals _____

2. a likeness of a person _____

3. worth more than any money that could be paid for it _____

4. without errors _____

5. changes _____

6. designs formed on wood or metal plates _____

7. pictures made by one of the earliest photographic methods _____

8. withdraw to escape from a battle _____

9. the workroom of an artist or a photographer _____

10. a place to see a display of pictures, art work, and sculptures _____

B. Antonyms are words with opposite meanings. Write each word below next to its antonym.

bright   excellent   popular   won   sell
started   advance   damage   few

1. restore _____

2. retreat _____

3. disliked _____

4. dim _____

5. purchase _____

6. defeated _____

7. poor _____

8. stopped _____

9. many _____

The Story of Matthew Brady and His Camera

Proper and Common Nouns

Nouns are words that name persons, places, and things.

A. Proper nouns are names of specific persons, places, and things.
Find the proper nouns in the story and write them on the lines below.

Persons	Places	Things
Matthew Brady	_____	_____
_____	_____	_____
_____	_____	_____
_____	_____	
_____	_____	
_____	_____	
	_____	

B. Common nouns name persons, places, and things too, but not specific ones.
Write a common noun from the story on each line below.

Persons	Places	Things
artists	_army camps_	_portraits_
_____	_____	_____
_____	_____	_____
_____	_____	_____
_____	_____	
_____		

Memory Books

Your best friend has moved to another city. Your grandparents or someone in your family lives far away. A friend or family member is sick. How do you keep in touch? A memory book is a great way to let people know you are thinking about them. You can fill your book with photographs, artwork, funny stories, or a summary of what's going on at home or at school. It will be a treasure for someone to read over and over.

To put together a six-panel book, you need a piece of paper that measures 36" by 8" (90 x 20 cm). Any sturdy paper or brown wrapping paper will fold into an accordion book. You need to measure and cut the paper to the right size.

1. collect supplies _____

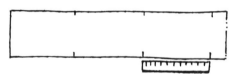

2. measure _____

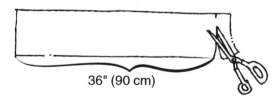

36" (90 cm)

3. _____

Next, measure to divide the book into six sections. Each section will be 6" (15 cm) wide. Mark the pages at 6", 12", 18", 24", and 30" (15, 30.5, 45.5, 61, and 77 cm). Mark along both the top and bottom of the book so that you can fold evenly on the lines.

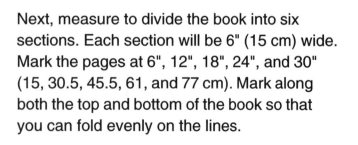

4. _____

Carefully fold at each mark. Fold the paper like an accordion. Fold the first page to the right and the second page to the left. The folding pattern is right, left, right, left, right, left.

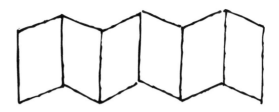

5. _____

Use a hole punch to make two holes in the center (near the outside edge) of the first and the last page.

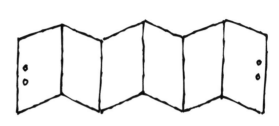

6. _____

String a piece of yarn, or a narrow piece of package ribbon, through the holes on the first page. The loose ends of the yarn will hang down the first page. Gently wrap the yarn around the book and through the two holes on the back page. Thread the yarn through the front holes and tie a bow. Your book is finished. Well, it's almost finished.

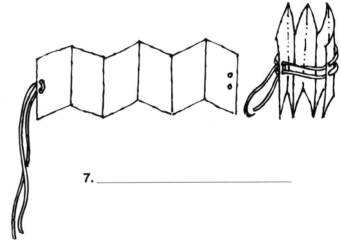

7. _____

The rest is up to you. It's time to create your masterpiece. First, choose a subject. Write the title and the author's name (that's you) on the cover. You might write about your soccer team, a field trip, or a family trip to a state park. Family members like to see pictures of themselves and read about family get-togethers.

You have six pages to decorate. You can draw, paint, or put together a collage. You can decorate the outside cover of your book too.

Your book can be mailed in a special mailing envelope.

If you had fun making this book, you can make memory books for birthday and holiday gifts for your family. The students in your class could work together to make holiday books for people in rest homes. Memory books create a lot of smiles.

Name _____

Questions about *Memory Books*

1. Use an action word (verb) to label all of the pictures in the directions for making the memory book. The first two pictures are labeled for you.

2. List all the supplies you need to make a memory book up to the point of decorating it.

   _____   _____

   _____   _____

   _____   _____

3. What supplies would *you* use to decorate your memory book?

   _____

   _____

   _____

4. Number the steps for making a memory book in order.

   _____ Punch two holes in the first and last pages.

   _____ String yarn through the holes.

   _____ Measure and cut the paper.

   _____ Fill the pages with art and writing.

   _____ Gather all your supplies.

   _____ Accordion-fold the paper.

Name _____

Memory Books

Apply What You Learned

1. To whom would you send a memory book? Why?

   _____

   _____

2. Make a list of four possible topics for memory books.

   _____   _____

   _____   _____

3. Choose one of the topics, and write and illustrate a page for that memory book.

Name _____

Memory Books

Verbs and Adverbs

1. When you follow directions, a lot of **action verbs** tell you what to do.
   The action verbs are underlined in the following phrases:

   <u>string</u> a piece of yarn   <u>wrap</u> the yarn   <u>thread</u> the yarn

   Find five more action verbs in the story that tell you what to do. Write them on the lines.

   _____   _____

   _____   _____

   _____

2. Other verbs in the story show a **state of being** or are **helpers** added to an action verb.
   The following underlined words are examples from the story:

   family member <u>is</u> sick   <u>could</u> work

   Find three words in the story that help action verbs. Write each word and its action
   verb partner on the lines.

   _____   _____

   _____

3. **Adverbs** are words that tell how an action is done. Some adverbs end with the
   letters **ly**. Find the following adverbs in the story. Write the verb that each describes.

   gently _____   _____ evenly

   carefully _____

   Write a sentence of your own using each of these adverbs. Underline the action word
   in your sentence.

   _____

   _____

   _____

Memory Books

Syllables

Here are 15 words from the story. Count and write the number of syllables in each word.

memory	_____	holiday	_____	measure	_____
narrow	_____	decorate	_____	panel	_____
masterpiece	_____	summary	_____	collage	_____
treasure	_____	accordion	_____	envelope	_____
photograph	_____	create	_____	author	_____

Word Meaning

Find words in the list above that match these definitions. Write each word by its definition.

a. a work of art made with objects and pieces of various materials _____

b. a part or a section _____

c. a shortened account of a story or an event _____

d. a great work of art or music _____

e. to bring into being _____

Now find the words listed above in the word search.

```
H N Z T L B A Z R F N T E E N D P
A O K M A N M E A S U R E M T S R
C A L C Z L E T L K Z B A N C E D
C T P I B J M A S T E R P I E C E
O U A D D C O L L A G E H D H G O
R S U M M A R Y X D E C O R A T E
D W T G N J Y P H J B W T N N Z N
I S O P L C R E A T E L O A P H V
O L W C T P S T X N H J G D S W E
N A R R O W H T Z O E L R D T M L
V X T R E A S U R E L L A B J D O
U R M D P A U Q V L Y T P B N N P
K V M O Z T A K C A U T H O R E E
```

The Harmony Zoo Times

Animal Skyscrapers

Giraffes are the tallest living land animals in the world today. The height of female giraffes averages about 14 to 16 feet ($4\frac{1}{4}$ to 5 meters), and males average 16 to 18 feet (5 to 6 meters). Giraffes weigh from about 1,800 to 3,000 pounds (810 to 1,360 kilograms).

These peaceful giants have necks that are six to eight feet ($1\frac{3}{4}$ to $2\frac{1}{2}$ meters) long. Where the neck joins the head, there is a special joint the giraffe can use to lift its head so that it is in a straight line with the neck. The head, when pointing straight up, adds another two feet (60 centimeters) to the height of the giraffe. Even though the giraffe's neck is longer than the necks of other animals, it has only seven vertebrae. That's the same number of neck bones that humans have.

The giraffe's legs are twice as long as its body. The front legs of the giraffe are longer than the back legs. The giraffe's back slopes downward slightly from the shoulders to the back legs. With these extraordinary legs, the giraffe can walk 10 miles (16 kilometers) in an hour.

When it's in a hurry, it can gallop at speeds up to 35 miles (56 kilometers) an hour. The head and neck move back and forth when the giraffe walks and runs, which helps this tall animal balance and move more quickly.

A giraffe's heart must work hard to pump blood up the neck to the brain. The heart that does all this work is about two feet (60 centimeters) long and weighs about 24 pounds (11 kilograms). The blood vessels in the brain and special valves in the arteries in the neck control the flow of blood so that it doesn't rush to its head when the giraffe lowers its neck.

Giraffes have very good eyesight. They can see something moving over a mile away. Sometimes one giraffe will keep watch while other giraffes lower their heads to drink water. Other grazing animals come to the water hole when giraffes are drinking because they know their tall neighbors can see trouble coming a long way off.

Giraffes, like cattle, are ruminants. Their stomachs have four sections. Food, mixed with saliva, is swallowed whole. Then

© David R. Bridge

the giraffe brings up a lump of food, chews, and swallows it again. The food is digested when it reaches the fourth stomach.

Acacia leaves are the giraffe's favorite food. The leaves are about three-quarters water and provide moisture when there aren't any lakes or water holes nearby. The giraffe's tongue is about 18 inches (45 centimeters) long. The length of the tongue makes it easy for a giraffe to reach the tops of acacia trees and pull off small leaves. The sharp thorns surrounding the leaves don't bother giraffes.

Every giraffe has its own

unique color pattern. Some giraffes have large, straight-edged spots that are close together. Others have irregular spots that can be jagged or smooth. A few giraffes are a single color.

A giraffe's short hair always looks clean even though the giraffe doesn't bathe. Instead, it licks its body. With its long tongue, it can even clean its nose and ears. Oxpecker birds help groom the giraffe. These birds walk up and down the giraffe's back, eating insects and getting rid of dried skin and loose hair.

A newborn giraffe stands about $6\frac{1}{2}$ feet (2 meters) tall. Its neck is very long compared to its body. While she goes away to eat, the mother giraffe hides her baby in tall grass to protect it from predators such as lions. Few lions or other animals attack a young giraffe when the mother is near. She strikes them with her strong hooves. Her blows injure the attacking animal so badly that it can't harm the young giraffe.

After the first month of life, all the young giraffes in the herd

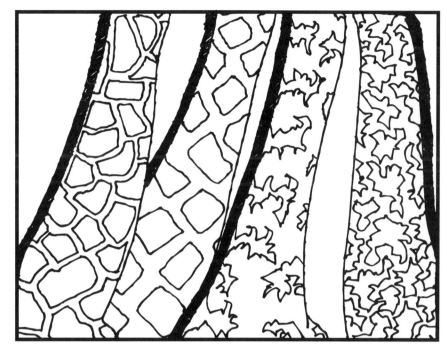

Every giraffe has its own unique color pattern.

are left together in a sheltered area while the mothers search for food. Sometimes a baby-sitter is left with the young giraffes. Young giraffes play games and gallop after each other while they wait for the return of their mothers.

There are a number of threats to giraffes. The human population is growing in central Africa, where most giraffes live. Both giraffes and people need more land. The people need food, and giraffes can provide large quantities of meat. In the past, too many giraffes were killed for their hides, tail hair, and meat. Droughts and disease have also reduced the number of giraffes.

Other factors favor the future of giraffes, however. Farmers and

© David R. Bridge

herders have learned that giraffes don't eat the same grasses that cattle eat. Sometimes giraffes can be seen eating tree leaves while cattle graze around them. Giraffes don't usually eat the crops people grow.

These amazing animals attract tourists from all over the world. The tourists spend money. They need food and places to stay when they come to see the giraffes. This means more jobs for Africans.

Today there are laws to protect giraffes, and some land has been set aside for giraffes and other animals. If giraffes are to survive outside of zoos, people must continue to preserve giraffe habitats and find ways to protect these gentle giants.

Questions about *Animal Skyscrapers*

1. Write four facts from this article that contain measurements of length and weight.

2. What traits do giraffes have that help protect them?

3. Why do other animals come to the water holes to drink when they see the giraffes are there?

4. How do oxpeckers help giraffes? How do the giraffes help the oxpeckers?

5. The human population in central Africa is growing. How does this affect giraffes?

6. How are tourists helping to save the giraffe population?

7. What is being done to help giraffes?

Name _____

Animal Skyscrapers

Topic Sentences and Supporting Details

1. In the outline below, each of the sentences states the main topic of one of the paragraphs in the article. Under each sentence, write the facts in the paragraph that tell about the main topic. List these supporting facts in as few words as possible. You do not need to write complete sentences. The first one is written for you.

Giraffes

I. Giraffes have good eyesight.

    A. Can see something move over a mile away

    B. _____

II. Every giraffe has its own color pattern.

    A. _____

    B. _____

    C. _____

    D. _____

III. Giraffes, like cattle, are ruminants.

    A. _____

    B. _____

    C. _____

    D. _____

2. The supporting details below are taken from one of the paragraphs in the article. Write a topic sentence on the line.

I. _____

    A. Licks its body

    B. Can clean its ears and nose with long tongue

    C. Oxpecker grooms giraffe

        1. eats insects on giraffe

        2. gets rid of dried skin and loose hair

Name _____

Animal Skyscrapers
Vocabulary

1. Write these words on the lines following their definitions.

extraordinary	blood vessels	ruminant	moisture
irregular	habitat	graze	crops

a. plants grown in fields by farmers _____

b. tubes in the body where blood flows _____

c. an uneven shape _____

d. exceptional; extremely unusual _____

e. a cud-chewing animal _____

f. where an animal lives _____

g. water or liquid _____

h. to feed on growing grass _____

2. What word in the article means a person who travels away from home to visit

   different places? _____

3. Write the word from the article that means to run rapidly. _____

4. Write the word from the article that means a person who cares for and watches cattle

   or other grazing animals. _____

Animal Skyscrapers

Prepositions

A **preposition** is a word that is placed before a noun or a pronoun. It shows the relationship of that noun or pronoun with some other word in the sentence. For example, when we say "a basket for the eggs," the word *for* is a preposition. It shows the relationship between *basket* and *eggs.* The group of words *for the eggs* makes up a **prepositional phrase**.

Here are some prepositions that you read all the time:

in	on	at	with
under	for	near	above
behind	around	through	without
of	over	beneath	near
from	before	between	during
about	after	below	off
until	to	by	among

Find six prepositional phrases in the article and write them below. Circle the preposition in each phrase.

_____

_____

_____

_____

_____

Holidays in India

The people in India celebrate many holidays. Many religions are practiced in India, and every religion has holy days and festivals. Muslims, Sikhs, Buddhists, Christians, Hindus, and Jains celebrate their own religious holidays throughout the year. The different religious groups celebrate national holidays and many special days together.

A family day set aside for brothers and sisters is very popular. On that day, a sister ties a bracelet on her brother's wrist. This special gift is called a *rakhi* [rah - kee]. It's believed that the rakhi will protect the brother from harm during the coming year. The sister puts a small circle of red powder on the brother's forehead, and there are special treats. Brothers give presents to their sisters and make a pledge to care for them.

Diwali is a festival of lights that takes place in October or November. It honors Lakshmi, the goddess of wealth and beauty. Stores and houses are cleaned and decorated with lights. The streets and buildings sparkle with row after row of lights. During the festival, it's believed that Lakshmi brings good luck to well-lighted places. People visit each other and partake of special foods throughout this three- to five-day celebration.

The Holi celebration in March is one of India's most colorful holidays. People throw colored chalk and water on friends and strangers as they walk along the streets. People sing, dance, and enjoy the entertainment.

Animals are given great importance in India and take part in many Indian holidays. There is a festival for the snakes that live in the temples. People bring them milk and flowers on their special day. During the Pooram festival, which takes place in the spring, elephants are painted and decorated with gold and brightly colored patterns.

When it's time for Ponggal, people celebrate to give thanks for the rice harvest and for the rains. A clean, freshly painted house and new clothes are important preparations for the festival. Colored rice powder and chalk are used to paint designs inside and outside of the house.

Celebrants prepare ponggal, a sweet, candied food made from rice, milk, and brown sugar. An offering of ponggal is set out for the gods. Later, people share the ponggal. People leave other gifts on the altars, including food, oil, incense, and clay models of horses. Their offerings thank the gods for the rains and the rice harvest. Money is given to help keep the temple in repair.

Indians consider cattle sacred. During Ponggal, cattle are honored for their work during the year. These animals help farmers by pulling the heavy plows through the rice fields. On the third day of the festival, the cattle are bathed. Their horns are often painted blue and gold. Rings of flowers are draped around the cattle's necks and colorful feathers are tied around their heads. After the cattle are decorated, they are paraded and given some of the ponggal as a treat.

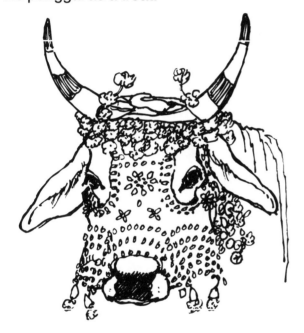

An exciting contest is held during the festival. Money is tied around a bull's neck and on the bull's forehead. Men try to take the money from the bull without being injured by the bull's horns.

On January 26, people in India celebrate Republic Day. That is the date on which, in 1950, India was granted independence from Great Britain. Animals line up with people for the Republic Day parade in New Delhi. The elephants' trunks are covered with painted flowers. Camels and horses are groomed and adorned for the parade. Uniformed and costumed people and decorated animals travel from many parts of India to march along the parade route. The president and crowds of people watch the show.

Many villages in India hold fairs called *melas*. People come from long distances to buy, trade, and sell. There are many shows and dances. A camel fair is held in the town of Pushkar every year. At this fair, camels are traded, raced, and even participate in beauty contests. Vendors sell many goods, including saddles and supplies for camels. In the evening, people sing around campfires.

Festivals, melas, and holy days are important parts of life in India throughout the year. ∎

Questions about *Holidays in India*

1. What customs do brothers and sisters follow on Brother and Sister Day?

_____

_____

_____

2. Why are houses and buildings well lit during Diwali?

_____

_____

_____

3. What is the reason for the celebration of Ponggal?

_____

4. Why are cattle honored during Ponggal?

_____

_____

_____

5. Describe the Republic Day parade in New Delhi.

_____

_____

_____

6. What happens at a *mela*?

_____

_____

_____

7. How can you tell that animals are important in India?

_____

_____

_____

Name _____

Holidays in India

Mapping Information

Make a map about the following holidays in India. Write at least two details under each of the holidays listed.

Brother and Sister Day	Diwali

Holidays in India

Ponggal	Republic Day

Holidays in India
Vocabulary

A. Fill in the blanks using words from the story.

1. What word means almost the same as patterns? _____

2. What word means types of faith or worship? _____

3. Write the word that means a tool for making rows in a farmer's field.

   _____

4. Write the word that means the activities that take place to get ready for an event.

   _____

B. Write these words on the lines by their definitions.

ponggal	harvest	holy	goddess
pledge	popular	route	rakhi

1. a special bracelet given by sisters to their brothers _____

2. honored by a church or religious group of people; sacred _____

3. the gathering of crops from the fields _____

4. the path or road followed to travel from one place to another

   _____

5. something liked by many people _____

6. a candied food made with rice, milk, and brown sugar _____

7. a promise _____

8. a female deity _____

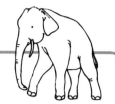

Holidays in India
Vocabulary

Fill in the spaces in the crossword puzzle using words from the list.

Across

1. a colorful holiday where people throw colored water on each other
3. Indian day of independence
4. sellers
8. worthy of great respect, holy
9. a festival of lights
12. a festival where cattle are honored
13. cows and bulls

Down

1. celebrations
2. an animal that is often used to carry people and supplies in the desert
5. large animals with trunks
6. a time of celebration; a special event
7. to observe a day with special events and festivities
10. reptiles
11. an Indian fair

Word Box						
cattle	celebrate	snakes	camel	Republic Day	festival	sacred
Holi	vendors	elephants	holidays	mela	Diwali	Ponggal

Snug Harbor Times
Sports Review

Home Run Summer

Sports records are made and broken every year, but in the summer of 1998, the number of baseball home runs turned the sports world upside down. Home run kings Sammy Sosa and Mark McGwire slugged their way past the record seasons of Babe Ruth and Roger Maris. Babe Ruth blasted 60 home runs over stadium walls and into the stands in 1927. No one topped that record until Roger Maris batted 61 home runs in 1961. During the past 129 years in baseball no major league player hit more than 61 home runs in one season.

In 1998 thousands of Chicago Cubs fans watched Sosa tally up 66 home runs before the play-offs. It was an incredible feat, but it was five homers short of the 1998 record. Sosa played home-run tag with St. Louis Cardinal Mark McGwire all season. Two days before the last game, Sosa was ahead by one home run. He had sent a record 66 balls beyond the playing field. McGwire had a total of 65. Before McGwire headed home at the end of the season, he had chalked up 70 home runs. Five of those record-smashing homers came during the final weekend of the season. On September 27, McGwire slammed his 69th and 70th home runs in the last game against the Montreal Expos.

"To say the least, I'm amazed," McGwire said. "Hitting 70? I've never thought about it, or dreamt about it. When I got to 62 early in September, everybody said, 'Shoot for 70.' I'm speechless, really. I can't believe I did it. Can you? It blows me away."

How did it all happen? By August 7, McGwire had bashed 45 home runs with Sosa close behind at number 43. Less than a month later, McGwire added 10 more runs for a total of 55. On September 8, McGwire tied Maris's record of 61 homers and went on to break the tie the next night. Even more

dramatic, the record-breaking hit came during a game with the Cubs. McGwire hugged his son, Maris's children, and Sammy Sosa. Five days later, in Chicago, Sosa hit his 62nd homer in a game with the Brewers. What did he have to say about his record-tying home run? "It's unbelievable," Sosa exclaimed.

Sosa and McGwire weren't the only major league players with winning bats. Other season power hitters were Ken Griffey, Jr. of the Mariners with a total of 56, the Padres' Greg Vaughn with 50, and Albert Belle of the White Sox, who connected for 49. In 1998 the total number of major league home runs added up to 5,064, the highest total for the past 16 seasons. The Cardinals socked 223 home runs out of the park—the best team record in the National League. What did the season's home-run mania do for baseball? Neither the Cardinals nor the Cubs were in the World Series in spite of their ball-bashing ways. Home run excitement boosted baseball attendance. Fans packed the baseball stadiums to see the action, and more visitors made visits to Baseball's Hall of Fame to learn about baseball's past record setters. In Mark McGwire's words, "I think the magnitude of this probably won't sink in for awhile. This is a season I will never, ever forget, and I hope nobody in baseball ever forgets it."

Other near record-breaking news from the major leagues came from the New York Yankees. People were so busy thinking about home runs, they almost overlooked the Yankees' winning streak. The Yankees won 114 games that season. The only team to top that record was the Cubs with 116 wins way back in 1906.

Babe Ruth

Herman "Babe" Ruth joined the New York Yankees in 1920. In four different seasons he hit more than 50 home runs. In 1927 he belted 60 homers out of the park. He was the first major league player to hit more than 24 home runs in a season. His career home run total was 714, a record he held for 40 years. Hank Aaron broke Ruth's record by ending his career with a total of 755 home runs.

Before Ruth gained fame as a power hitter, he was a left-handed pitcher with the Boston Red Sox. In 1915, his rookie season, he won 18 games. The next two years he pitched even more winning games. Ruth set a record for consecutive scoreless innings in World Series play. He was such a powerful hitter that he was needed in all the games. Because pitchers are not in the line-up every day, Ruth's managers decided to change his position. Ruth proved to be an excellent fielder as well as a pitcher.

Some of Ruth's nicknames were the King of Clout, the Sultan of Swat, Bambino, and Bam.

Roger Maris

Roger Maris was a left-handed batter and an outstanding outfielder. He played with many major league ball clubs. In 1961 he hit 61 home runs, breaking Babe Ruth's record. He tallied up his record-breaking number of home runs in 162 games. Ruth achieved his 60 home runs in a 154-game season. Maris received the Most Valuable Player award for the American League in 1960 and 1961.

Questions about
Home Run Summer

1. Write the single-season home run records that are mentioned in *Home Run Summer*. Record them in the order in which they happened.

   _____

   _____

   _____

2. Who was the first major league player to have more home runs during his career than Babe Ruth?

   _____

3. How did the home run race between Mark McGwire and Sammy Sosa help baseball?

   _____

   _____

4. What advantage did Roger Maris have when he broke Babe Ruth's record?

   _____

5. In 1998 the New York Yankees came very close to breaking a major league record set in 1906. What was the record and how close were they?

   _____

   _____

6. Even though McGwire and Sosa set baseball records, their teams were not in the 1998 World Series. Why do you think that happened?

   _____

   _____

   _____

Home Run Summer

Think about It

1. Sammy Sosa and Mark McGwire showed good sportsmanship even though they were competing. What clues did you read in the article that supported this?

   _____

   _____

   _____

   _____

2. Who will break Mark McGwire's home run record? Will it be you? Write a newspaper article about the event. Be sure to include the future date in your article.

   _____

   _____

   _____

   _____

   _____

   _____

   _____

   _____

   _____

Home Run Summer

Vocabulary

A. Find each word below in the article. Read the sentence in which the word is used.
Use the sentence context to help you understand what the word means.
Write your own definition.

1. magnitude: _____

2. mania: _____

3. nickname: _____

4. boosted: _____

5. consecutive: _____

6. tallied: _____

7. incredible: _____

8. dramatic: _____

B. Read *Home Run Summer* again. Find at least four verbs that are used in place of the word *hit.*

_____   _____

_____   _____

Name _____

Home Run Summer

Write a Summary

Write a brief summary of the article *Home Run Summer*. Use as many of the words in the word box as you can.

Word Box				
Babe Ruth	Hank Aaron	Sosa	McGwire	consecutive
amazed	boosted	stadium	tallied	major league
mania	incredible	home run	Maris	dramatic

_____

_____

_____

_____

_____

_____

_____

_____

_____

_____

_____

_____

_____

Rachel Carson

It might have been possible to predict Rachel Carson's eventual career when she was a child. Even then she loved to write. She won awards and prizes for her stories when she was 10 years old. Three of her stories were published in a magazine called *St. Nicholas*.

Rachel was an outstanding student. When she finished high school, she studied at Pennsylvania College for Women. At first, she majored in writing and English. After taking an exciting science class in biology, she decided to change her studies and learn more about science. Rachel continued to write for the college newspaper and had stories published in the school's literature magazine. She graduated in 1928 with honors and went on to earn a master's degree in zoology at Johns Hopkins University.

Rachel Carson, 1907–1964

While Carson was a student, she worked as a laboratory assistant at Woods Hole Marine Biological Laboratory. There she observed and learned about life in the ocean.

Even with scholarships and help from the universities, it was hard to earn enough money to stay in school. During the 1930s many people were jobless. Factories closed because people didn't have enough money to buy the factories' products. More workers lost their jobs. Carson's family, like others in the United States, had very little money. She taught university classes in biology to help pay for her education.

Rachel loved teaching science and studying about the ocean. She wrote poems and stories about nature. She tried to sell what she wrote to magazines. She was unsuccessful except for articles accepted by *The Baltimore Sun*, a Maryland newspaper.

Carson's father died in 1935, and she had to find a way to support herself and her mother. The Bureau of Fisheries in Washington, D.C., wanted a writer who was a marine biologist to write radio programs about the sea. It was a temporary job, but it would pay $1,000 for a year's work. She decided to take the job and work for the government.

When Rachel's sister died, her two daughters came to live with Rachel and her mother. Rachel needed a permanent job to support her new family. She took a test to qualify for a government job and received the highest score. In 1936 she became a full-time employee with the Bureau of Fisheries. Her salary increased to $2,000 a year.

Carson's poem "Undersea" was published in 1937 by the *Atlantic Monthly* magazine. A publishing company asked her to write a book based on the poem. Her book, *Under the Sea Wind,* was completed right before World War II. People were busy working and helping the government during the war. Not many people wanted to buy a book about the sea at that time.

Even though her book wasn't successful, Rachel continued to write. Much of her writing was for bulletins and government publications about fish.

After the war, Rachel wrote another book entitled *The Sea Around Us.* It became a best seller. She won many awards. People then became interested in reading her first book too. Her third book was entitled *The Edge of the Sea.*

There were many changes happening in Rachel's life. One of her nieces died, and Rachel adopted her niece's five-year-old son. The following year, Rachel's mother died.

Carson's last book was entitled *Silent Spring.* She wrote about the effects of the pesticide DDT on people and animals. At first DDT did stop mosquitoes and insect pests. Then some of the insects became immune to the poison and didn't die. DDT doesn't decompose or disappear quickly when insects are exposed to the poison. Other animals sicken and often die when they eat the insects or animals that have the pesticide in their bodies.

Rachel described how DDT harmed wildlife, the environment, and people. She showed that birds with DDT in their systems laid fewer eggs. Eggs in their nests were thin-shelled and broke easily. Some of the hatchlings didn't live or were deformed.

Companies that produced pesticides denied DDT was harmful, but people wanted to know the truth. Scientists gathered more information that showed Carson's research was scientifically accurate. The careless use of pesticides was harmful to animals and people.

The president and people in Congress studied the reports. Eventually laws were passed that banned the use of DDT in the United States. Carson's book was one of the first warnings about the contamination of our environment. Her writing made people realize that the careless use of chemicals and waste products from factories could harm the earth.

Rachel Carson died in 1964 of cancer. Years later, her adopted son accepted the Presidential Medal of Freedom in her name from President Carter.

Questions about *Rachel Carson*

1. Why did Rachel Carson decide to change her course of studies in college?

   _____

2. What was the subject of Carson's first three books?

   _____

3. In *Silent Spring*, Carson warned people about the pesticide DDT. How does the use of DDT harm the earth?

   _____

   _____

   _____

4. Why do you think the companies that produced DDT denied it was harmful?

   _____

   _____

   _____

5. What was the result of Rachel's book *Silent Spring*?

   _____

   _____

   _____

6. What could have happened if Rachel hadn't written *Silent Spring*?

   _____

   _____

   _____

Name _____

Rachel Carson

Think about It

Although Rachel Carson sounded the warning about dangers to our environment over 50 years ago, there are still problems to be solved.

Write about what you think are the dangers facing the environment today. Do you think we can solve these problems? How?

_____

_____

_____

_____

_____

_____

_____

_____

_____

_____

_____

_____

_____

Rachel Carson

Vocabulary

1. Write the letter of each word on the line in front of its definition.

   a. biology   _____ having to do with the sea
   b. pesticide   _____ a gift of money or aid to help a student pay for school
   c. laboratory   _____ the scientific study of living organisms
   d. marine   _____ a place for scientific study
   e. scholarship   _____ a chemical for destroying insects

2. Circle the correct meaning for these words in the story.

   a. salary   lettuce and tomatoes
                       money earned for work
                       a big sale

   b. employee   a person hired to work for another
                       not having a job
                       a bookcase

   c. temporary   very hot
                       not for a long time
                       unpleasant

   d. permanent   ending tomorrow
                       lasting forever
                       changing

   e. environment   surroundings
                       a type of work
                       pesticides

3. Write the two words in section 2 above that are antonyms.

   _____   _____

4. Find the 13-letter word in the story that means "the act of making impure or unfit for use."

   (Hint: It begins with a "c.")   c _____

Name _____

Rachel Carson

Suffixes can change the meaning of the base or root word. Study each ending below and its meanings. Then write a definition for each word that contains the suffix. For example:

> **ist**—one who studies or practices
>   zoologist—a scientist who studies animals
>   scientist—a person who practices the scientific method
>   biologist—a scientist who studies living things

1. **ness**—state of being

       carelessness _____

2. **en**—to make or become

           sicken _____

3. **ly**—in a way that is

           scientifically _____

4. **ful**—full of

           harmful _____

           successful _____

5. **less**—without

           harmless _____

           jobless _____

6. **ment**—a state of, or having to do with

           environment _____

           government _____

7. **ee**—a person who is

           employee _____

KidKrafts Magazine
Napkin Rings for Any Occasion

Just think of all the times during the year when your family sits down to special meals—there are birthdays, Thanksgiving, Valentine's Day, and so many more celebrations. Wouldn't it be fun to have napkin rings to decorate the table for each event? Here's how you can make them.

How to Make Napkin Rings

You will need paper towel rolls, paper, wrapping paper, self-adhesive paper, or plain paper that you have decorated, any extra decorations you want to add, glue, scissors, a pen or a pencil, and a ruler.

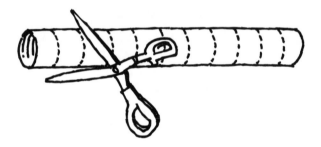

Place the ruler on the paper towel roll. Make a mark at every inch (2.5 cm). Place the scissors on each mark and cut. Count the rings. Are there enough for everyone in the family and guests? If there isn't one for every person, cut another roll.

If you are using plain paper to cover the rolls, decorate the paper before you cut it. Cut a strip of wrapping paper or self-adhesive paper that measures $2\frac{1}{2}$ inches (6.5 cm) wide and $5\frac{1}{2}$ inches (14 cm) long.

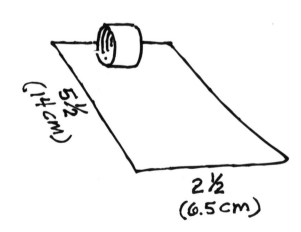

5½ (14cm)

2½ (6.5cm)

Rub glue on the outside of the roll, unless you are using self-adhesive paper, which has its own glue. Center the $5\frac{1}{2}$-inch (14 cm) strip of paper around the outside of the roll. The ends will overlap.

 Read and Understand, Nonfiction • Grades 4–6 • EMC 749

There is $\frac{3}{4}$ inch (2 cm) of paper left over on each side of the roll. Make cuts in the paper on each side of the roll—about every $\frac{1}{2}$ inch (1.5 cm). Lightly glue both inside ends of the roll.

Add ribbon or decorations to the outside of the napkin ring. When the special day comes, tuck napkins, paper or cloth, into the rings and set them by the plates on the table. After dinner, put the rings in a bag in a "Special Days" box that you've prepared. They'll be ready for the next birthday or the same holiday next year.

Keep the Fun Going

As each new special celebration approaches, make a new set of napkin rings for the table. Next year you will have a collection of napkin rings for the whole year in your Special Days box. Then you'll have time to plan more decorations for family celebrations.

Keep a box of paper scraps and reusable items like the paper towel rolls or egg cartons and plastic tubs. Add ribbons and pieces of holiday wrapping paper. Use your imagination to come up with decorating ideas made with the materials in the box. There are many craft books in the library to help you think of new ideas.

Spread the Fun Around

Everyone will look forward to your holiday surprises. If friends and family ask to help with the decorations, celebrate with a work party. Have all the materials ready for the projects you decide to do. Be sure to have a few cookies, punch, and soft music (so you can talk to each other and show off your artwork). These extras will make your work time as special as the holiday decorations you are preparing. You may even need a second decoration box to store all your work. Have fun!

Name _____

Questions about
Napkin Rings for Any Occasion

1. List the materials needed for making napkin rings.

   _____   _____

   _____   _____

   _____   _____

   _____   _____

   _____

2. If you use self-adhesive paper, what item in the list of materials isn't needed?

   _____

3. What other decorations could you make for special days at home?
   Select one of your ideas and write the directions for making that decoration.
   Make a list of all the materials you need for the project.

Materials List: _____   _____

                       _____   _____

                       _____   _____

                       _____   _____

Steps to Follow:

_____

_____

_____

_____

Name _____

Napkin Rings for Any Occasion
Sequencing

Number the directions in order.

A. _____ Count the rings.

_____ Place the scissors on each mark and cut.

_____ Make a mark at every inch.

_____ Place the ruler on the paper towel roll.

_____ Make extra rings.

B. (You will complete this part. See below.)

C. _____ Glue the inside of the roll.

_____ Glue the inside of the roll again.

_____ Make cuts in the paper on each side of the roll.

_____ Bend one side of the paper to the inside of the roll and press down.

_____ Bend the other side of the paper to the inside of the roll and press down.

The directions given above are not complete. Four steps are missing in section B. Write them in order on the lines.

1. _____

2. _____

3. _____

4. _____

Napkin Rings for Any Occasion

Tell What You Think

1. What is your favorite day of the year?

   _____

2. Why do you like it more than other holidays or celebrations?

   _____

   _____

   _____

3. Do you think that decorations made by the family would make celebrations more special? Explain your answer.

   _____

   _____

   _____

4. List some of the foods your family prepares and eats on holidays.

   _____

   _____

5. How could your favorite day be made more fun or interesting? Give some ideas for things you and your family could make and do.

   _____

   _____

   _____

   _____

Name _____

Napkin Rings for Any Occasion

Following Directions

Follow the directions below and use the information provided to create a celebration calendar for some interesting events.

You will need:
- 12 pieces of white paper
- some good ideas
- marking pens, paints, or crayons

Directions:
1. Label each page with the date and description of an event given below.
2. List some ways to celebrate each special day.
3. Illustrate your celebration calendar.

January 18, 1882—The birthday of A. A. Milne, who created Winnie-the-Pooh.

February 2—Groundhog Day (If the groundhog sees its shadow, it will be a long winter. If there is no shadow, spring will arrive soon.)

March 31, 1889— Alexandre Gustave Eiffel completed the Eiffel Tower for the Paris World's Fair. At that time it was the tallest building in the world.

April 13, 1796—The first Indian elephant came to North America (New York City).

May 25, 1895—George Herman Ruth, one of the greatest baseball players in the major leagues, was born. His nickname was Babe.

June 4, 1896—Henry Ford drove his first Ford automobile in Detroit, Michigan.

July 1—Canada Day. Canadians celebrate the forming of the Dominion of Canada.

August 26, 1920—Women won the right to vote.

September 16—Mexican Independence Day. On this day in 1810, Miguel Hidalgo y Costillo gave his *grito*, or call for revolution, to free Mexico.

October 24—United Nations Day. The United Nations is an organization of countries that promotes peace and health throughout the world.

Tuesday following the first Monday in November—Election Day in the United States.

December 12, 1901—Guglielmo Marconi amazed the world by sending the first radio signal across the Atlantic Ocean.

City of Mystery

About 30 miles northeast of Mexico City are the ruins of a great city. No one knows the name of the city, what language the people spoke, or who built its great pyramids. Archaeologists, detectives of the past, are trying to dig up the facts. Every day they uncover more clues that will help them solve the mystery, but they haven't found the answers to these questions.

They know that around 100 B.C. there were small villages scattered throughout the area. Seventy-five thousand people lived in the city 300 years later. By A.D. 600 twice as many people lived here. It had grown into one of the largest cities in the world.

The Aztecs, who settled where Mexico City is today, arrived hundreds of years after the city had been destroyed. When they discovered the ancient city, no one lived in the apartment complexes or walked along the magnificent Avenida de los Muertos. The Aztecs named this place the City of the Gods, Teotihuacán. They didn't believe that ordinary people could have built the pyramids and the buildings they found. The Aztecs made pilgrimages to the ancient city to pray. They searched the ruins for artifacts made by the people who had lived there. They found stone masks and pottery, but there was nothing made of metal. The knives and tools

The Avenue of the Dead
and the Pyramids of the Sun and the Moon

they discovered were fashioned from obsidian and stone. There were no wooden objects and cloth left because they had disintegrated with time.

The Aztecs marveled at the two gigantic pyramids that towered above the city. They named them the Pyramid of the Sun and the Pyramid of the Moon. The Pyramid of the Sun is the largest. It is as tall as a 20-story building (65.5 meters), and the base of the pyramid covers 500,000 square feet.

The people who lived in this mysterious city studied the stars, the planets, and geometry. Their buildings, for example, were built so the walls faced north, south, west, and east. Specially marked stones show that the people measured and used the position of the solar system and stars to plan their streets and buildings.

About 60 to 100 people lived in each apartment complex in the city. Their living quarters were arranged around a patio. Altars were set in some of the patios so people could leave offerings and pray to their gods.

There were many foreigners, people from other areas of Mexico, who lived there. Artifacts found in the apartment areas show that they came from long distances to live in this great city. Perhaps they were artisans who made objects to trade, or people who came there to live because of the marketplace.

Teotihuacán was a great trading center. Traders traveled there with a variety of goods from faraway places. Elegant bird feathers, chocolate, vanilla, pottery, salt, fish, and obsidian were probably exchanged in the marketplace. Other valuable items included nose plugs and earrings carved from jade, polished obsidian mirrors, stone images of the feathered serpent god, the storm god, and the great goddess. Jointed pottery dolls and stone masks could have been offered for sale too. While people bargained and exchanged goods, large pottery vases by the temples burned incense that perfumed the air.

Murals, huge paintings on the walls, have been found in buildings and underground chambers. The signs on the paintings show that the people in Teotihuácan probably had a system of picture writing.

There were many ceramic figures of people unearthed in the city. Were these 1,500-year-old faces modeled from the citizens or from important people? It's one of the questions archaeologists and anthropologists are trying to answer.

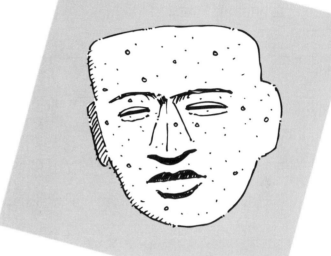

Will all the questions about this great city be answered one day? Scientists, archaeologists, and anthropologists are working together to find out more about Teotihuacán. They haven't given up. Perhaps one day they'll find more pieces to this ancient puzzle. If you decide to become an archaeologist and dig up the past, you could be the one to solve the mysteries of Teotihuacán. ∎

Questions about
City of Mystery

1. Who named the city Teotihuacán? What does the name mean?

   _____

   _____

2. How tall is the Pyramid of the Sun? How much ground does it cover?

   _____

   _____

3. Why is Teotihuacán called the City of Mystery?

   _____

   _____

4. Why do you think archaeologists didn't find any metal in the city?

   _____

   _____

5. Would you want to have lived in Teotihuacán? Explain your answer.

   _____

   _____

   _____

6. What do you think happened to Teotihuacán and the people who lived there?

   _____

   _____

   _____

City of Mystery
Vocabulary

A. Write the number of each word on the line in front of its meaning. Use story clues or a dictionary to help you.

1. anthropologist   _____ very old

2. archaeologist   _____ City of the Gods

3. Teotihuacán   _____ a large structure with four triangular-shaped sides

4. artifact   _____ the remains of a building or city that have fallen down

5. pottery   _____ journey made to a special religious place

6. disintegrated   _____ bowls and pots made of clay

7. pyramid   _____ an object made in an earlier time

8. pilgrimage   _____ a person who studies people and their cultures

9. ancient   _____ decayed

10. ruins   _____ a person who studies objects and buildings from the past

B. Find these missing words in the story and write them on the lines.

1. In 100 B.C. many groups of people lived in different places near Teotihuacán.

   Their houses were s_____ around the area.

2. Some of the artisans who lived in the city made c_____ figures.

3. Archaeologists found many paintings called m_____.

4. F_____ , people who came from other places, lived in the city of Teotihuacán.

5. The signs on the paintings in the city could mean the people of Teotihuacán had

   a system of w_____ with pictures.

         Read and Understand, Nonfiction • Grades 4–6 • EMC 749

City of Mystery

Prefixes

Prefixes are special sets of letters that are added in front of a base (root) word. Prefixes can change the meaning of the word.

A. Sometimes the prefix **un** means "not." For example:
      kind means to be nice to or thoughtful of others
      unkind means to be mean or not thoughtful of others

  1. Add the prefix **un** to each underlined word in the following sentences and then rewrite the sentence. You may need to change more than one word.

     a. The mysteries of Teotihuacán have not been <u>solved</u>.

     _____

     b. It is not <u>clear</u> who the people of Teotihuacán were.

     _____

  2. Find two words in the story with the prefix **un**. Write them on the lines next to their definitions.

     _____ taken out of the earth

     _____ to find; take the cover off

B. The prefix **dis** often gives the base (root) word the opposite meaning or means to take away. For example:

      discolor means to change or spoil the color

  1. Find a word in the story with the prefix **dis** that means "found something that

     has been hidden or unknown." _____

  2. Find a word in the story with the prefix **dis** that means "broke up, fell apart,

     and decayed." _____

Name _____

City of Mystery

Use Your Imagination

It is 300 years in the future. You are an archaeologist who is digging on the site where your school is now located.

Draw a picture or a map that shows what you discovered.
Write a paragraph describing what you found.

Love That Chocolate!

Drop a spoonful of powdered chocolate in your milk. Dribble chocolate frosting on your graham cracker or celebrate a holiday with coins wrapped in gold foil, a chocolate Santa, or a cream-filled egg. Even better, open a box of aromatic chocolates—after dinner, of course. Wait! Even if you ate all your vegetables, don't scoop up a handful. Take a deep breath, or two, or three. Enjoy the tantalizing smell. Next, survey the chocolate rectangles and circles. Which ones hide your favorite creams, nuts, or caramels? No fair poking holes in the bottoms of the candies to find the one you want. Be adventurous. Take a chance and bite into the one in the middle of the box. Try again if it's not what you expected, but remember to save some for tomorrow.

Where does all this chocolate come from? Read on to find out.

Chocolate for Sale

Chocolate comes from cacao trees grown on large plantations. When chocolate is harvested, it doesn't have the same mouth-watering flavor you discover when you bite into a chocolate chip cookie. A lot of processing is needed to get that marvelous chocolate taste.

Pods of chocolate beans hang from the trunk, not from branches of the tree the way apples do. Blossoms form on the trunk throughout the year. The football-shaped pods that develop from the flowers are harvested whenever they're ripe. It takes five to six months for the pod to change from green to a ripe, purple color.

Inside each pod are 20 to 40 white seeds (beans) that are about the size of almonds. The seeds are surrounded by white pulp. The pulp

The cacao tree is native to the eastern coast of Mexico. Now it is grown all over the world in the tropical zones near the equator. Usually the cacao tree enjoys the shade of other trees. It thrives where the temperature never drops below 60°F (16°C), and prefers year-round temperatures in the 80s (27° to 32°C). If it's grown on plantations, it's pruned to 25 feet (8 meters). In the wild it can grow to 50 feet (15 meters) and live about 60 years.

and seeds are cut out of the pods. Then the bitter-tasting seeds and pulp are either placed in boxes in the hot sun or heated. The beans grow and die. The heat turns the pulp into liquid that is drained from the beans. After the beans are thoroughly dried, they turn a dark chocolate

 Read and Understand, Nonfiction • Grades 4–6 • EMC 749

color and are shipped to candy factories all over the world. The smell and flavor from these beans is similar to the sweet odor of chocolate in a candy bar, but the beans aren't ready yet.

Chocolate at Last!

In the factories, chocolate beans are brushed clean, roasted, and crushed into particles called *nibs*. The outer shell isn't thrown away. It's used for fertilizer or food for cattle.

The nibs are ground into a hard brown block of cocoa. During the crushing process, liquid cocoa butter may be extracted from the beans. Some of the crushed nibs and cocoa butter are used in lotions and soaps.

Different types of rich chocolate, depending on the amount of cocoa butter, remain. Will it be processed into baking chocolate? It could be added to sugar and candy fillings for chocolate bars or candies that melt in your mouth. Maybe it will flavor a truckload of Rocky Road ice cream. Some of the chocolate will be added to bitter medicines to make them taste better.

Chocolate in Your Diet

Chocolate bars are very rich and will add a lot of calories to your diet. One small chocolate bar has about the same number of calories as two bananas or one-third pound of cheese. Eating half of a loaf of bread will add only a few more calories than a candy bar.

During World War II, the Hershey company made candy bars for soldiers to add extra calories and energy to their diets. Some explorers in cold climates eat chocolate to help them stay active. Chocolate bars are a good source of minerals and vitamin B, but chocolate, like coffee, contains caffeine, which can keep you awake when your body needs rest.

Chocolate Conquers the World

Long before people in Europe settled in the Americas, the Native Americans enjoyed chocolate. It was made into a special drink for royalty. The Aztec kings added chocolate to a mixture of seasonings and corn mash to make a bitter, peppery beverage. Sometimes honey, vanilla, and peppers were added. Chocolate was so valuable that it was used as money in the marketplace.

When Spanish ships carted chocolate beans back to Spain, it became a popular drink with the royal family and the nobles in the Spanish court. Sugar was added to the drink. Wooden beaters were used to whip the chocolate until it foamed. Orange water, white rose powder, cloves, and other spices were mixed into the chocolate.

The Spanish tried to keep chocolate a secret, but eventually visitors to the royal court took the drink back to their own countries. In the 1600s, its popularity spread across Europe. A hundred years later, chocolate was shipped from England to the English colonists in North America. The colonists became very fond of chocolate drinks. Their doctors prescribed chocolate for energy and good health. ■

Questions for *Love That Chocolate!*

1. At what time during the year are chocolate beans harvested?

   _____

2. How long does it take for a pod of chocolate beans to ripen?

   _____

3. Could you grow a cacao tree where you live? Why or why not?

   _____

   _____

4. Before the Spanish came to Mexico, the Native Americans who lived there made a special drink with chocolate. How else did they use chocolate beans?

   _____

5. What ingredients did the Spanish use to make chocolate drinks?

   _____

   _____

6. In what section of the food pyramid does chocolate belong?

   _____

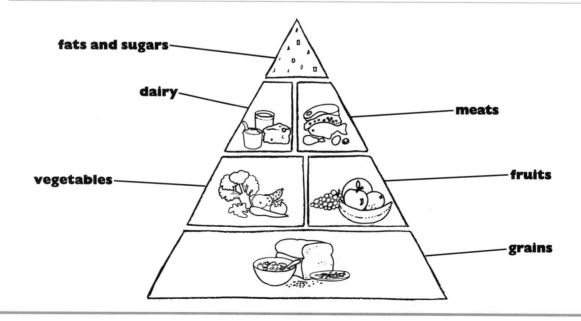

Love That Chocolate!
Vocabulary

A. Search the story for the words to fill the blanks in the following sentences. The number of blanks tell you how many letters are in each word.

1. Cacao trees grow best in the ___ ___ ___ ___ ___ ___ ___ ___ zones of the earth.

2. The ___ ___ ___ containing the chocolate beans grows on

   the ___ ___ ___ ___ ___ of the tree.

3. When cacao trees grow on plantations, they are ___ ___ ___ ___ ___ ___ so they don't grow as tall as they do in the rainforests.

4. The outer coating of the bean is used for

   ___ ___ ___ ___ ___ ___ ___ ___ ___ ___ and cattle food.

5. A chocolate bar has as many ___ ___ ___ ___ ___ ___ ___ ___ as two bananas.

6. The cacao tree ___ ___ ___ ___ ___ ___ ___ in areas where the temperature never drops below 60°F and stays in the 80s.

7. The seeds are surrounded by white ___ ___ ___ ___.

8. When the seeds are harvested, they have a ___ ___ ___ ___ ___ ___ taste.

B. What word in the second paragraph of the story means "very fragrant"? _____

C. How many words can you think of to describe the smell, taste, and appearance of chocolate? Write the words under the best heading.

Smell	Taste	Appearance
_____	_____	_____
_____	_____	_____
_____	_____	_____
_____	_____	_____
_____	_____	_____

Name _____

Love That Chocolate!

Follow Directions to Play a Game

You need:
- a partner
- four 3" x 5" (7.5 x 13 cm) index cards
- pencil
- scissors
- a die
- two game markers
- game board

How to get ready:
1. Fold the index cards in fourths.
2. Cut on the folds to make 16 cards.
3. Write one word on each card. You will need to use four of the words twice.

survey	pods	nib
processed	calories	prescribe
cacao	plantation	equator
tropical	harvested	pulp

How to play:
1. Turn the cards over and mix them up.

2. You and your partner each choose eight cards.

3. Place the cards face down.

4. Roll the die to decide the first player. The highest number begins.

5. The first player rolls the die and moves his or her marker that number of spaces on the board.

6. If he or she has a word that matches the definition written in that space, the word card is placed on the space. If the player cannot match the definition, the next player rolls the die.

7. If a player lands on a space covered by a word card, he or she goes to the next space.

8. The winner is the player to run out of cards first.

Love That Chocolate!
Game Board

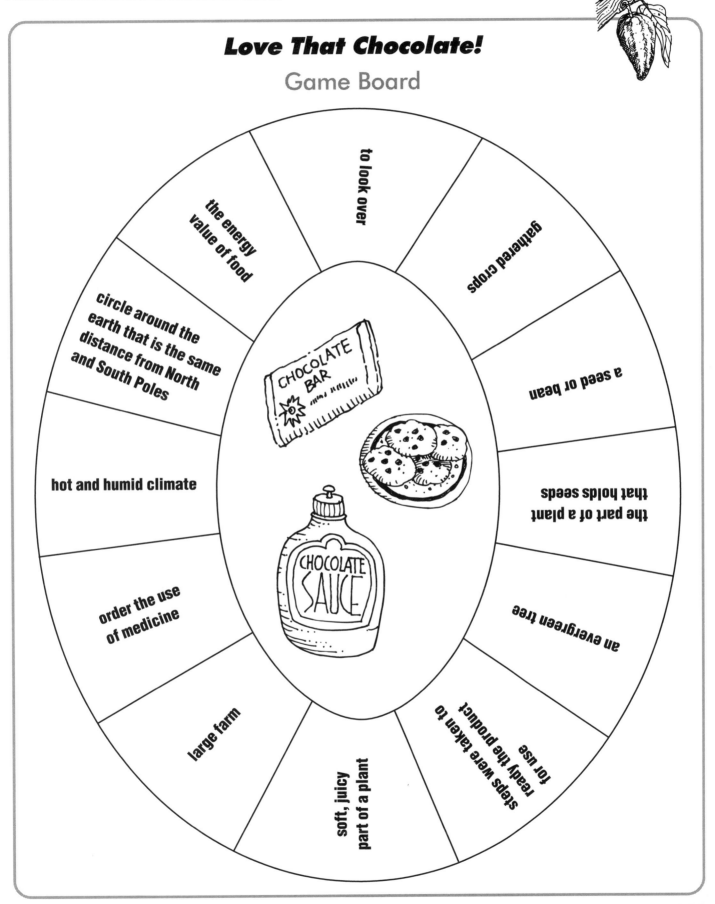

to look over

the energy value of food

gathered crops

circle around the earth that is the same distance from North and South Poles

a seed or bean

hot and humid climate

the part of a plant that holds seeds

order the use of medicine

an evergreen tree

large farm

steps were taken to ready the product for use

soft, juicy part of a plant

Toads

Toads and frogs belong to the group of animals called amphibians. The word *amphibian* comes from Greek and means having two lives. Both toads and frogs really do live two lives. First as tadpoles, they hatch from the eggs and live in the water. They undergo changes (metamorphosis) in the water. When they have their adult frog and toad bodies, most become land animals. They return to the water to lay their eggs.

Frogs and toads are so much alike that scientists often classify toads as a type of frog. Toads differ from the other frogs in their family because they have rougher skin and shorter hind legs. They have bumps, or tubercules, on their bodies. Toads are heavier than other frogs, and with their short hind legs, they can't hop as far. Many toads have glands on the sides of their neck. They give off a toxic fluid when the toad is attacked. Snakes don't seem to be bothered by the toxins, but most other animals quickly let go of the toad when they taste this poison. Toads can be as small as 1 inch long (2.5 cm) or as large as 9 inches (23 cm).

Toads are nocturnal animals. During the day they hide in dark, damp places. Where winters are cold, they bury themselves in the ground in the winter and hibernate until the weather is warmer.

Toads absorb moisture through their skin instead of drinking it. When the weather is too hot, they can cover up underground where it is moist and estivate until the weather cools.

Toads feed on beetles and other insects, grubs, worms, and slugs. The 9-inch-long (23 cm) marine toads in Texas and Florida are big enough to eat mice. The toad has a long tongue attached to the front of its mouth. This sticky tongue darts out to catch insects flying nearby.

Toads swallow in an unusual way. They blink their eyes each time they swallow. Because there are no bones between the eye and the mouth, the eye presses against the roof of the mouth when it blinks. This pushes the food into the body.

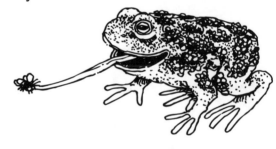

Toads lay eggs in pools of water. A strip of gelatinlike material that can be more than four feet long surrounds the eggs. The amount of time it takes the eggs to develop and hatch depends on the species of toad. It can take several months for the tadpoles to grow legs and develop into toads.

Read and Understand, Nonfiction • Grades 4–6 • EMC 749

Midwife Toad

The Midwife Toad

The midwife toad is found in southwestern Europe. The male takes care of the eggs. After the female lays the eggs, the male wraps the strings of eggs around his thighs. Each night he moistens the eggs with pond water or dew. After a month, he takes the eggs to the pond. Tadpoles leave the eggs and swim away.

Surinam Toad

This tropical toad can grow to 6 inches (15 cm). It is a brown or gray color like many other toads. It has webbed hind feet, and its front legs have star-shaped tips on the ends. This toad lives in the water and eats small fish and other water creatures. The male presses the eggs onto the back of the female. Her skin makes a pocket around each egg. The tadpoles swim away once they hatch from the eggs.

Spadefoot Toad

Spadefoot toads have smooth skin. Usually they don't have the toxin glands found on other toads. The name "spadefoot" comes from the tubercules on each hind foot. This 2-inch-long (5 cm) toad uses these special hind feet to dig into the earth. It can quickly hide under the ground. In fact, the spadefoot stays underground most of the time. After a spring rain, spadefoots head for newly created ponds to lay their eggs. Because the water can dry up quickly, spadefoot tadpoles become toads in a few weeks and head for land. Many spadefoots are killed by cars when they cross roads on their way to and from the ponds.

American Toad

The American toad can be found in the Eastern United States and Canada. It is 1 to 2 inches long (2.5 to 5 cm). The colors of the American toad vary, but generally it is a brownish olive. The musical trilling songs that come from an external vocal pouch can identify the males. The tadpoles leave the eggs after only three days. After two months they hop out of the pond in their adult bodies, ready to live on land.

Fowler's Toad

Unlike the melodic American toad, this amphibian screams out its song. It's found in the same area as the American toad. Fowler's toads don't have spots on their bellies and chests like the American toad. ■

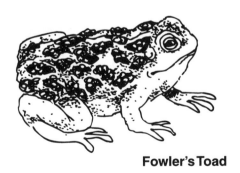

Fowler's Toad

Name _____

Questions about *Toads*

1. In what ways are toads different from frogs?

   _____

   _____

2. How do the toads' eyes help them swallow?

   _____

   _____

3. How does the location of a toad's tongue help it catch food?

   _____

   _____

4. Why do toads return to water?

   _____

   _____

5. List the unusual characteristics of the spadefoot toad.

   _____

   _____

   _____

6. What are the differences between the Fowler's toad and the American toad?

   _____

   _____

   _____

Toads
Vocabulary

1. Find the word in the story that means the physical changes the toad goes through from

   egg to adult. _____

2. Many toads have glands that give off a poisonous fluid. What other word used in the
   story means "poisonous"? Then write the noun form of that word meaning "poisons."

   _____   _____

3. You are probably familiar with the word *hibernate,* which means "to sleep or rest in
   the winter." What word in the story means "to sleep or rest when the weather is hot"?

   _____

4. Fill in the blanks using the best words from the story.

   a. The American toad has a very pleasant song. It is _____.

   b. The vocal cords of the American toad are in an _____
      pouch.

   c. Toads hunt for food at night. They are _____.

   d. Toads lay eggs in a string of _____.

5. What is the Greek meaning of the word *amphibian*?

   _____

Name _____

Toads

Make an Information Map

There are many ways to write and organize information when you need to remember what you read. One way is to make a map. Use the information in the story to complete this map about the Surinam toad. Write words or phrases, not whole sentences.

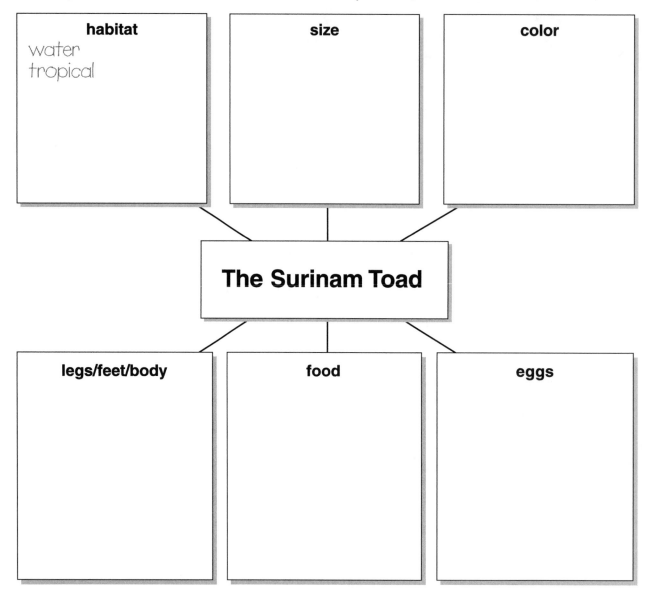

habitat
water
tropical

size

color

The Surinam Toad

legs/feet/body

food

eggs

Bonus: On another paper, make a map about the American toad using the same headings as the ones for the Surinam toad. (Clues: To find the food the American toad eats, look for the kinds of foods most toads eat. To finish the description of the color, look under Fowler's toad.)

Name _____

Toads
Crossword Puzzle

Complete this crossword puzzle using words from the story *Toads*.

Across

2. poisonous
5. changes in form, such as caterpillar to butterfly
6. the outer covering of a toad
7. a toad with a musical voice
8. a bump or a growth
11. on the outside
12. active at night
13. to be dormant in the summer

Down

1. a toad with star-shaped tips on its front feet
2. amphibians with bumpy skin and short hind legs
3. animals that live on land and in the water
4. to be dormant in the winter
8. relating to the zones of the earth nearest the equator
10. the place where an animal lives

Vietnamese Holidays

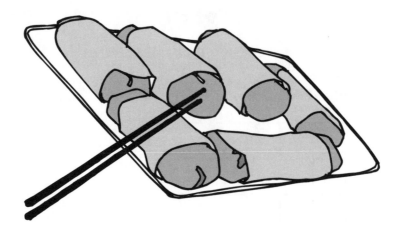

The Vietnamese celebrate many festivals during the year. There are special days set aside to remember ancestors and their spirits. There is an incense ceremony day and a long list of national holidays. On almost every special day, there are parades, prayers, flowers, fireworks, and holiday foods.

During an autumn festival, children parade with lanterns. Everyone eats moon cakes, a pastry filled with sesame or bean paste, and admires the harvest moon.

Buddhists, the followers of Buddha, celebrate his birthday every year. Captive birds and fish are set free in his honor.

One of the most important celebrations is Têt, the Vietnamese New Year. Almost everyone in Vietnam honors this holiday. Têt begins on the first day of the lunar year and signals the beginning of spring. Têt doesn't come on the same day every year because the date for Têt depends on the cycles of the moon. The festival takes place on different dates in January or February and lasts from three to seven days.

Before Têt begins, the home is cleaned and decorated with spring blossoms. Banners and lights are hung outdoors. People try to be kind to everyone. It's important to settle arguments that have taken place during the year.

Têt is a time to honor ancestors. An altar with pictures of the ancestors is arranged in the home. Food is set out on the altar along with candles and incense. The family invites the spirits of their ancestors to share the New Year's Eve dinner.

The Kitchen God is honored with a special offering to make him happy. At the end of each year, he is thought to give reports about the family to the Jade Emperor in Heaven. If the Kitchen God is pleased, the family believes he will praise them.

At midnight the family prays for good health and good fortune in the New Year. Loud strings of firecrackers are set off to chase away the evil spirits.

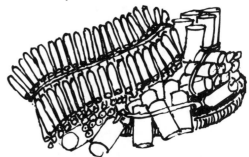

On the first day of the New Year, people go to the temples and pagodas. They pray to the gods of their religion. They pray for their ancestors and ask for a good new year. Children receive presents of red envelopes with money inside. The family enjoys special treats of preserved fruit and lotus seeds.

It's believed that the first visitor to the house during Têt brings good luck or bad luck for the coming year. The family takes great care to invite a special person to the house who will bring them good fortune.

Many holiday foods are served during Têt. Some favorites are sweet rice cakes with beans, noodles, fruits, and dumplings filled with pork and green beans.

Many small villages in the hill country celebrate Têt with traditional songs and dances from their region. They have special New Year activities like horse races or wrestling matches.

After the Têt celebrations, spring has officially arrived. It's time to plant crops and spring rice. ■

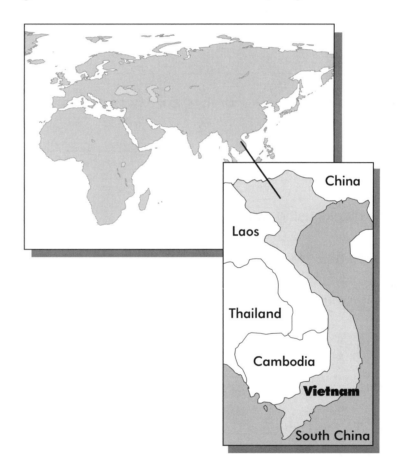

Name _____

Questions about
Vietnamese Holidays

1. Why doesn't Têt begin on the same day each year?

   _____

   _____

2. Why are offerings set out for the Kitchen God?

   _____

   _____

3. How do the Vietnamese honor their ancestors during Têt?

   _____

   _____

4. Fill in the blanks using words from the story.

   a. Têt takes place in _____ or _____ .

   b. Têt lasts from _____ to _____ days.

   c. During Têt, it's important to be _____ to everyone and

      settle _____ .

   d. Before Têt, the house is _____ and _____ with

      spring _____ .

5. Why is it important to invite a special guest to visit during Têt?

   _____

   _____

Vietnamese Holidays

Vocabulary

A. Find these words in the story.

1. List the names of two places where people in Vietnam go to pray.

   _____   _____

2. What is the word that means a substance that produces a sweet smell when burned?

   _____

3. What word means relatives in your family that lived long ago?

   _____

4. What is the name of steamed dough filled with bean paste and other foods?

   _____

B. Write these words next to their definitions.

lotus	preserved	altar	national
spirits	cycle	Tết	ceremony

1. belonging to a country _____

2. a water plant that produces a seed that can be eaten _____

3. a place to pray and leave offerings _____

4. ghosts _____

5. religious or public activity with a special purpose _____

6. a period of time or an event that is repeated many times _____

7. processed to last a long time _____

8. the name of the New Year celebration in Vietnam _____

C. Name five foods mentioned in the story. _____

Name _____

Vietnamese Holidays
Main Topics and Details

The following are topics found in the story. Write details under each of the topics.
Write one fact by each letter.

I. Kitchen God

    A. _____

    B. _____

    C. _____

II. Altars

    A. _____

    B. _____

    C. _____

    D. _____

III. Buddha's Birthday

    A. _____

    B. _____

IV. Autumn Festival

    A. _____

    B. _____

    C. _____

V. The First Day of the New Year

    A. _____

    B. _____

    C. _____

    D. _____

    E. _____

Name _____

Vietnamese Holidays
Word Search

A. Find these words in the word search.

Vietnam	altar	ancestors	sesame	banners	Têt	plant
fortune	rice	temples	spring	lights	honor	

```
M  R  D  V  C  R  M  B  U  J  D  X  E  O
P  J  X  I  W  T  B  T  G  T  P  M  Z  N
D  R  G  E  E  R  A  I  M  U  A  W  B  T
X  A  L  T  A  R  N  J  Q  S  O  L  A  R
P  L  A  N  T  I  N  C  E  F  E  E  L  H
K  T  U  A  N  C  E  S  T  O  R  S  I  G
Z  L  T  M  G  E  R  S  P  R  I  N  G  T
T  E  M  P  L  E  S  Z  K  T  S  L  H  E
S  O  L  G  M  P  W  E  R  U  M  O  T  S
T  C  W  E  X  L  R  H  O  N  O  R  S  T
P  X  S  Z  B  J  X  H  K  E  M  L  N  H
```

B. Choose two words in the word search and write a sentence about Vietnam for each word.

_____

_____

_____

_____

Games People Play Magazine

The Greatest Athlete in the World: The Story of Jim Thorpe

Jim Thorpe and his twin brother, Charlie, were born in Oklahoma. His father was Irish and Native American from the Sac and Fox tribes. His mother was Potawatomi. They lived on a farm on the Sac and Fox reservation.

Thorpe learned to work on the farm. Even though the family worked hard, there was always time for athletic games. His father taught him how to hunt and fish.

Thorpe's father wanted him and his brother to have a good education. When the boys were six, he sent them to a reservation boarding school 25 miles from home. It was a U.S. government school for Native American children.

Thorpe didn't want to go to school, but he stayed because he liked the sports he and his brother played with the other students.

Charlie became ill with pneumonia when the boys were eight. There were few doctors near the reservation and no antibiotics to help people with pneumonia and diseases at that time. Charlie, Jim's brother and best friend, died. Jim wanted to stay home after that, but his father insisted he return to school. He ran away from the school several times and came home.

Then his father sent Jim to a school for Native Americans that was farther away in Kansas. There, Jim learned to play football. When his father was injured in a hunting accident, he traveled home, 270 miles on foot. His mother died while he was at home, and Jim was needed to help on the farm. He didn't return to Kansas.

James Thorpe, 1888–1953

Thorpe went to another school for Native Americans in Pennsylvania. At Carlisle, he learned to play football, baseball, and many other sports. He competed in track-and-field events. He played under an outstanding coach, Glenn "Pop" Warner. Thorpe competed against students from the best schools in the United States and won. He led his Carlisle teammates to victory in football and in track-and-field events.

One summer, Jim played on a minor league baseball team to earn some money. After that summer, he went home to help on the family farm because his father had died.

But Jim missed the school and sports, so he returned to Carlisle in 1911. He led his teammates in a winning year in athletic competition. In 1912 he went to Sweden to compete in the Olympics. At the games he won the gold for the pentathlon and the decathlon. His record number of points in the decathlon was not surpassed for 20 years. King Gustav of Sweden proclaimed him the "greatest athlete in the world."

People everywhere congratulated Thorpe. President William A. Taft sent him a special letter.

Thorpe continued to excel at every sport he tried, including rowing. He bowled and played golf, tennis, handball, hockey, and billiards. He even learned to figure skate. In 1912 at Carlisle, Thorpe played another winning season of football—his favorite sport.

It was discovered that Thorpe was paid to play professional baseball that one summer. This was against the Olympics committee's rules. Thorpe's medals and awards were taken from him even though people all over the world protested. Writers in magazines and newspapers came to his defense. The athletes who won second place medals in the pentathlon and the decathlon refused to take Thorpe's gold medals. They said he was the greatest athlete. But the committee refused to return Thorpe's medals.

Jim had offers from many teams to play professional baseball. He signed with the New York Giants for $5,000. Even though he was an outstanding player, the coach seldom allowed him to play. Jim went on to play successfully with other teams.

After so many setbacks, these were happy years for Jim, his wife, and children. But tragedy struck again when his son became ill and died at the age of three. Soon after, Jim began playing football as well as baseball, and he was seldom home with his wife and three daughters. His marriage ended in divorce.

Eventually Jim married again and had three sons. He retired from baseball in 1928 and from football in 1929.

The next years were difficult. He tried different jobs. People took advantage of him, and he didn't manage his money well, giving much of it away. He tried acting in movies, but received very little money and few acting jobs. His second marriage also ended in divorce.

Thorpe's third wife helped him keep track of his money. In 1950 the Associated Press honored him as the greatest football player. He received another award as the greatest athlete in the first half of the twentieth century.

After Jim Thorpe died in 1953, the Olympics committee returned his medals from the 1912 Olympics to his family. ■

Name _____

Questions about
The Greatest Athlete in the World

1. Why do you think Jim Thorpe liked Carlisle?

   _____

   _____

2. What medals did Thorpe win at the 1912 Olympic Games in Sweden?

   _____

3. Why were Thorpe's Olympic medals and records taken away from him?

   _____

4. Do you think it was fair of the committee to take away Jim's gold medals? Why or why not?

   _____

   _____

5. What professional sports did Jim play after he left Carlisle?

   _____

   _____

6. Write a two- or three-sentence summary of Jim Thorpe's life.

   _____

   _____

   _____

   _____

Name _____

The Greatest Athlete in the World
Vocabulary

A. Write each word by its definition.

pneumonia	competed	excel	professional	amateur
committee	disqualify	tragedy	protested	

1. a person who earns money for a job or a sport _____

2. a group of people who work together on a specific task _____

3. an illness _____

4. objected _____

5. to be superior to others in ability or quality _____

6. a person who takes part in a sport for fun rather than money _____

7. to take away rights or privileges _____

8. engaged in a contest _____

9. terrible or extremely sad event _____

B. Find the following phrases in the story. Read the sentence to let context help you determine the meaning. Circle the letter of the best definition.

1. took advantage of
   a. to unfairly try to gain money or privileges from someone
   b. to take the largest part of something
   c. to attempt to gain a first down in football

2. so many setbacks
   a. the distance the football is moved when a penalty occurs
   b. a big defeat or something that is in the way of success
   c. an enormous movement of earth

3. came to his defense
   a. to play a defensive position on a football team
   b. to serve in the army
   c. to argue for someone or help him or her

The Greatest Athlete in the World

A Word Game

The words below have missing letters. Read the clues that tell what the words mean and then write the missing letters. All the words are in the story. Skim the story and find the words to check your spelling.

1. a tract of land for Native American people   ___ ___ serv ___ ☐ ___ ___ ___

2. the process of gaining knowledge   ed ___ ___ ☐ ___ ___ ___

3. students live and learn there   ___ ___ ___ ___ ___ ing

     ___ ___ ___ ool

4. a contest with 5 track-and-field events   ___ ☐ ___ ___ ___ thlon

5. a contest with 10 track-and-field events   ___ ___ ___ ___ ___ ☐ lon

6. gained more than the amount   sur ___ ___ ___ ___ ___ ___

7. important   m ☐ ___ ___ ___

8. not often   s ☐ ___ ___ om

9. one hundred years   c ___ ___ tu ___ y

10. a gathering of athletes from many countries to compete for medals   O ☐ y ___ p ___ ___ ___

Now write the letters that are in the boxes above.

___ ___ ___ ___ ___ ___

Unscramble the letters to make a word that describes Jim Thorpe.

_____

The Greatest Athlete in the World

Organizing Information in an Outline

1. Fill in the missing parts in the outline.

   I. Home Life

      A. Was born in the state of _____

      B. Twin brother's name was _____

      C. Worked on the family _____

      D. Had time for _____

   II. At School

      A. Went to _____ school

      B. Didn't like _____

      C. Liked _____

      D. Brother died when he was eight

      E. _____ from school

2. Jim Thorpe was given an award for being the greatest athlete in the first half of the twentieth century. Write four facts from the story that tell why he was given that award.

   I. Named the greatest athlete in the first half of the twentieth century

      A. _____

      B. _____

      C. _____

      D. _____

Beak and Feather News

The tiny hummingbird can fly backwards and sideways.

The ostrich is the world's biggest bird. It can run 45 mph. An ostrich egg is bigger than a grapefruit.

All birds, from the giant ostrich to the tiny hummingbird, are warm-blooded vertebrates. They have two scaly legs, two wings, a beak, and feathers. Most birds molt once or twice a year. When they molt, they lose and replace all their feathers. The female bird lays eggs that are kept warm by one or both parents until the young birds hatch from the eggs. The parents feed the young until they are ready to leave the nest and hunt for their own food.

Birds live all over the world. Every species of bird has different habits and habitats. Each bird family builds the type of house that suits its lifestyle. Most birds fly, but a few, such as the ostrich, stay on the ground. Many birds migrate long distances to escape from cold winters. They don't carry maps or a compass, but they travel to the same place every year and seldom get lost.

Feet and beaks are adapted to the bird's lifestyle. Some birds have perching toes. Others have webbed toes that help them swim and keep them from sinking into the mud. Raptors have talons with sharp claws and very strong beaks. A seedeater's beak is different from the woodpecker's sharp, pointed drill. Bug eaters, mud probers, and fish scoopers have bills that help them find the kind of food they need.

Here's a closer look at four fascinating members of the feathered fellowship.

Owls

Owls are raptors–birds of prey–that hunt at night. These nocturnal meat eaters soar overhead looking for prey. With their sharp talons they can attack and carry off small ground animals.

Special fringed feathers on the edge of its wings make the owl's flight silent. A mouse or a

© Digital Stock

rabbit won't know the owl is near until it strikes.

The owl's large eyes can see even in the dark. It can see clearly far away and up close too. The owl sometimes looks like it has eyes in the back of its head. This is because it can turn its head in a half-circle to see directly behind itself. The owl's eyes don't move in the eye sockets, so its head must turn to see anything not directly in front of it.

© Digital Stock

Flamingos

This tall pink bird has a beak that acts like a sieve. It pokes its head into the water upside down looking for shrimp in the mud. The lower bill pumps out the water the flamingo scoops up. Algae and shrimp remain inside the beak. The pink coloring in the shrimp and algae passes through the flamingo's body and colors the feathers. Thousands of flamingos flock together in warm saltwater lakes and rivers.

Read and Understand, Nonfiction • Grades 4–6 • EMC 749

Males and females use their beaks to push mounds of mud into a nest.

© Digital Stock

Pelicans

This talented fisher has a pouch on its beak. The pouch can stretch to hold the fish the pelican catches. When the pelican spots a fish from the air, it dives at high speed straight down into the water.

When a pelican goes fishing, it takes in water along with the fish. With a beak full of water, it's too heavy to fly. Before the pelican can take off, it tips its head to the side to empty out the water. A grown pelican can eat 11 pounds of fish every day.

Parrots

There are over 300 kinds of parrots. Most parrots are green, but exotic blue, red, yellow, purple, black, and white parrots brighten the world's tropical rainforests too. The smallest member of the parrot family is the buff-faced pygmy parrot of New Guinea. It's just over 3" (7.5 cm) long. The largest is the hyacinth macaw in South America, which can grow to about $39\frac{1}{2}$" (1 m). Most of the macaw's length is in its long tail feathers.

The parrot's thick tongue and strong, curved beak help it eat nuts, fruits, and seeds. Some parrots use their beaks as a third foot when they climb trees. They have short legs and climb better than they walk.

Many parrots, like the African gray parrot, imitate the sounds of other birds. In captivity parrots can learn to talk. ■

© Digital Stock

Name _____

Questions about
Beak and Feather News

1. What features do all birds have in common?

   _____

   _____

   _____

2. What is unusual about the owl's head? Why is this unusual feature important?

   _____

   _____

3. Why are most flamingos pink?

   _____

   _____

4. After catching a fish, what does a pelican have to do before it can fly?

   _____

   _____

5. Tell about an unusual way parrots use their beaks.

   _____

   _____

6. Name the largest bird in the world. How large is its egg?

   _____

   _____

Name _____

Beak and Feather News

Vocabulary

1. Use the clues in the article to help you match these words and their meanings.

   vertebrates   molt   migrate   raptors
   sieve   exotic   captivity   talons

   _____ to move from one region to another

   _____ claws

   _____ the state of being held or imprisoned

   _____ strikingly uncommon, rare

   _____ animals that have an internal skeleton of bone

   _____ to shed feathers

   _____ birds of prey

   _____ perforated for straining liquids

2. Fill in the blanks using words from the article.

   a. Flamingos make mud nests in _____ and _____.

   b. The owl's eyes don't move in their _____.

   c. Many birds of the same species that fly and stay close together are called a

      _____.

   d. _____ toes help water birds swim and keep them from sinking into
      the mud.

   e. The tiny hummingbird can fly _____ and _____.

3. Circle the name of the bird that has a beak like a sieve.

   California condor   owl   eagle   flamingo   parrot

Name _____

Beak and Feather News

Summarizing Information

1. Read the first paragraph of the article. Write one sentence that summarizes what the information in this paragraph is about.

   _____

   _____

2. Read the second and third paragraphs. Write a one-sentence summary of the information contained in these two paragraphs.

   _____

   _____

3. Birds eat many different kinds of foods: fish, seeds, fruit, small animals, and insects. Write a sentence that states why this is so.

   _____

   _____

4. Reread about the following species of birds in the article. List one way in which each species is adapted to its environment.

   Parrots: _____

   Pelicans: _____

   Flamingos: _____

   Owls: _____

5. Choose your favorite bird named in the article. Tell why you chose this bird.

   _____

   _____

   _____

Name _____

Beak and Feather News

Using Apostrophes

Apostrophes are punctuation marks that look like this: '
Apostrophes are used in contractions such as **I'll**.
Apostrophes are used to show possession, as in the **child's** toy.

A. Find 12 words in the article that have an apostrophe. Write each word under the correct heading.

Contractions	**Possessives**	
_____	_____	_____
_____	_____	_____
_____	_____	_____
_____	_____	_____

B. Possessives can be singular—This is the puppy**'s** ball.
Possessives can be plural—These are the puppie**s'** food bowls.

Notice that when the plural noun ends with **s**, just the apostrophe is added. Complete the sentences with **s'** or **'s**.

1. The basketball game will be held in the boy_____ gym.

2. We quietly peered into the mother bird_____ nest in the oak tree.

3. That woman_____ hat is blocking my view of the parade.

4. You'll find the halters hanging next to the horse_____ stalls.

5. The player_____ mitts were lying on the bench.

6. Sara polished her brother_____ trophy.

Where in the World?

We're off on a mystery vacation. Use the map and the clues in the story to name our destination.

Pack your skis, snow gear, swimsuit, beach towel, and hat. Don't forget the sunscreen. We're heading south. We'll build giant sandcastles, admire the snow-covered Andes Mountains, and check out a few belching volcanoes. There's a very dry desert to cross. In some areas, rain never falls. We'll stop at a green desert oasis where warm springs supply water for plants and animals. We can take a side trip to an island with mysterious stone statues. Weather permitting, we'll cross icy waters to visit the land of the penguins. Watch out for icebergs!

When our boat docks at Arica, we'll spend a day or two on the beach. The ocean currents keep the temperature about the same all year. Our weather on this wintry August day is about the same as it would be on a summer day in December.

The country we are visiting is very skinny. We can leave the beach on the western coast in the morning, and arrive at a mountain resort near the eastern border in time to enjoy lunch.

There's no hurry, so let's take a detour. Instead of skiing today, we can travel about 100 miles (160 kilometers) northeast to Parque Lauca. We'll drive from sea level to an altitude of 13,000 feet (4,000 meters).

With our field glasses, we can spot giant condors flying overhead, find grazing vicuña, and track bounding long-eared rabbits. Lago Chungará, one of the highest lakes in the world, is a perfect place to watch flamingos and enjoy a picnic lunch.

Let's travel south when we leave the park so we can photograph herds of vicuña in neighboring parks. We'll need our swimsuits for a soak in one of the area's thermal hot springs.

Farther south we will have a close view of the smoking volcano, Guallatiri. Along the road are flocks of nandú.

Pink Flamingo

Vicuña

Andean Condor

Nandú

Animals seen during our mystery vacation.

Arica
Antofagasta
Easter Island
Viña del Mar
Valparaíso
Puerto Montt
Pacific Ocean
Parque Lauca
Lago Chungará
Volcán Guallatiri
Santiago
Atlantic Ocean
Punta Arenas
Antarctic Peninsula
Antarctica
Strait of Magellan

(Ben´ ya del mar), we'll head for mountain lakes. There'll be time for a river-rafting adventure on our way to Puerto Montt. After we hike around the lakes, we'll fly on to Punta Arenas, near the southern end of the country. It's located on the Strait of Magellan. It may rain, so carry your umbrella when you walk around the city. If it's a clear afternoon, our picture from the Cerro del Cruz will be a breathtaking souvenir of this southern city. The next day a cruise ship will take us to Antarctica to see a penguin rookery. It's the last stop on our visit to a South American neighbor. Adiós. ■

We'll drive west to Antofagasta, a port on the Pacific Ocean. From there, we'll take a plane to the capital city, Santiago. There isn't much time to tour the old Spanish-style churches and buildings in the city. Our bus leaves early the next morning for a skiing trip in the nearby mountains. After two days of fun in the powdery snow, we'll go on to Valparaíso. A ship is waiting there to take us on a long ocean voyage to Easter Island.

One of the best ways to travel around Easter Island is on horseback. It's very hot. Keep cool with a big straw hat and take out the camera. You'll want to snap pictures of the giant statues that are 18 feet to 22 feet ($5\frac{1}{2}$ to 7 meters) tall. There are many legends about the people who carved these statues. Just who they were is a real mystery.

After we return to Valparaíso and rest a day at the beach resort, Viña del Mar

Name _____

Questions about
Where in the World?

1. What country did you "visit" in this story? _____

2. List five clues that helped you guess the name of the country.

   _____

   _____

   _____

   _____

   _____

3. If you went to this country, which of the activities in the story would you enjoy the most? Explain your answer.

   _____

   _____

   _____

4. Why would you need to take different types of clothing to visit this South American country?

   _____

   _____

   _____

5. This is a very long, narrow country. What are the natural boundaries of the country?

   _____

   _____

Where in the World?

Vocabulary

1. Write the letter of each word on the line in front of its meaning.

   a. altitude   _____ an item kept as a reminder of a place visited

   b. strait   _____ the distance above sea level

   c. detour   _____ a strip of water between two larger bodies of water

   d. souvenir   _____ a roundabout way of going somewhere

   e. legend   _____ a breeding place of a group of birds or animals

   f. rookery   _____ an old story that explains what happened

2. Eight words in the story are compound words (two words connected together to form a new word). Write these eight words.

   _____   _____

   _____   _____

   _____   _____

   _____   _____

3. Fill in the blanks with these words to form the compound words.

   picks   flakes   soap   moon   tale   light   stage   mark

   _____suds   sun_____

   _____beams   _____coach

   book_____   tooth_____

   snow_____   folk_____

4. Choose one of the compound words you wrote above. Write a sentence for each of the two words that form the compound word. Write a third sentence using the compound word. Share your sentences with others in the classroom.

   _____

   _____

   _____

What Happened Next?

Reread *Where in the World?* As you read, draw a line on the map from one location to another to show the order in which places were visited. Begin with your arrival in Arica.

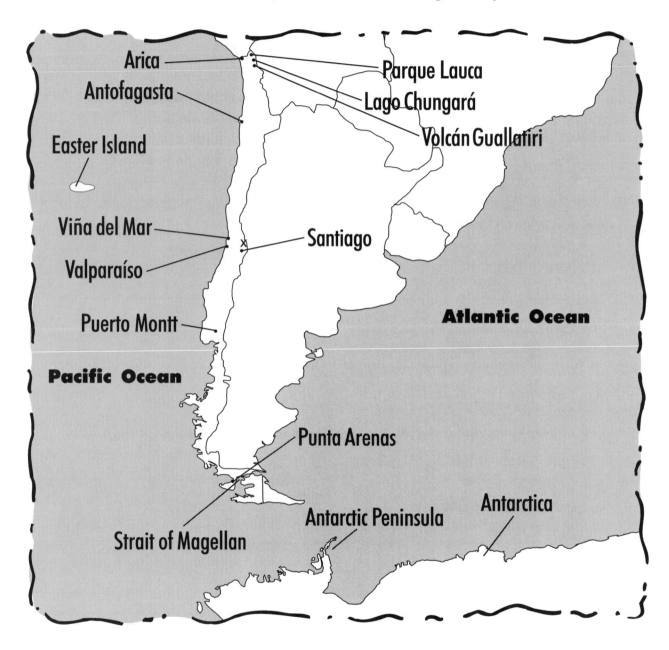

Arica
Parque Lauca
Antofagasta
Lago Chungará
Easter Island
Volcán Guallatiri
Viña del Mar
Santiago
Valparaíso
Puerto Montt
Atlantic Ocean
Pacific Ocean
Punta Arenas
Antarctica
Antarctic Peninsula
Strait of Magellan

 Read and Understand, Nonfiction • Grades 4–6 • EMC 749

Name _____

Where in the World?

Using What You Learned

Using what you learned about the country of Chile, design a travel advertisement or a poster inviting tourists to visit there.

Clouds

Clouds are nature's weather malls. They supply the earth with many styles of rain, snow, ice, and storms. Clouds regulate our solar heat. On a cloudy day, most of the radiation coming from the sun is reflected back toward space by the higher clouds. The radiation that passes through the clouds to earth is trapped between the earth and the lower layers of clouds.

Clouds form from water vapor. When solar heat causes water on the surface of the earth to evaporate, it travels up into the troposphere. (This is the 10-mile, 16-kilometer-deep layer of the atmosphere directly above the ground where weather happens.) When the tiny droplets of vapor bunch together, we see clouds in the sky. Some of the vapor freezes into ice crystals. The drops of water and ice crystals that make up a cloud are so light that they float in the troposphere. If they merge together, they become much heavier and fall quickly to earth.

All moisture, icy or warm, that returns to earth is called precipitation. Falling ice or snow crystals often melt in the warmer, lower atmosphere and turn into rain. If the lower air is cold, they fall as snow. Melting and refreezing ice crystals shower the earth with sleet.

Hail is made up of ice balls. Some are tiny, and others are the size of lemons. Gusts of wind toss the ice balls up and down like bouncing Ping-Pong balls. As they move through the air, more ice forms around the ice ball. When hailstones are too heavy to be supported by the air, they fall to earth. Hail can cause severe damage.

Name-Brand Cloud

There are more than 100 types of clouds. Clouds are classified by their color, shape, and position in the troposphere. There are high clouds, middle-level clouds, and low clouds. A fourth class of clouds has towering, vertical shapes that expand upward through all three levels of the troposphere.

The formation of the clouds is affected by how the air moves. If there is calm air, sheets of clouds cover the sky. When it's windy and the air is pushing upward, there are towering, billowy clouds.

Cumulus clouds are the woolly shapes that drift across blue skies. They are less than a mile above the earth. They are usually sighted on warm, sunny days. Cumulus clouds can grow and turn into cumulonimbus rain clouds. These towering clouds are called thunderheads. They cruise the airways at altitudes as high as eight miles above the earth. These moisture-saturated clouds are the source of heavy showers, thunder, lightning, and tornadoes. Another member of the cumulus family is the altocumulus cloud. They are dense, fluffy buckets of moisture that are two to four miles up in the sky.

Stratus clouds are low clouds. At night and in the early morning, stratus clouds sometimes rest on the ground as fog. When the sun warms the ground, the fog disappears. Stratus clouds cover the sky making it look gray. Stratocumulus clouds are wavy, lumpy clouds that are less than one mile up from the surface of the earth. They can send down a light drizzle or snow.

Cirrus clouds are high, swirling wisps of ice crystals. They are formed five miles or higher above the earth. Often, they have hooks or tufts on the ends. Because of this characteristic, they are sometimes called mare's tails. Cirrostratus clouds can be seen at night when they cover the moon with a thin, see-through haze.

Designer Clouds

Not all clouds are formed by nature. People are cloud-makers too. Contrails are one example. These strings of clouds are formed from the condensed water vapor from the exhaust of a jet airplane. Contrails add moisture and chemicals to the air. A large number of contrails add more cloud cover over the earth. Then the balance of sun and clouds is changed, and the weather can be affected.

Smog, a mixture of fog and smoke, is like a giant cloud that covers factories and cities. On smoggy days, it's harder to breathe. People have watery eyes. The pollution and chemicals they inhale irritate their lungs and throats. Buildings, rubber, and metal exposed to smog for long periods of time are damaged.

Cumulus Clouds

Stratus Clouds

Cirrus Clouds

Name _____

Questions about *Clouds*

1. How do clouds affect the weather?

_____

_____

2. How are clouds formed?

_____

_____

_____

3. Name two kinds of clouds made by humans.

_____

_____

_____

4. How are clouds classified?

_____

_____

_____

5. What is another name for a cumulonimbus cloud?

_____

6. Name four types of precipitation.

_____   _____

_____   _____

Clouds

Vocabulary

A. Use words from the story to fill in the blanks.

1. The heat from the sun causes the water on the surface of the earth to

   _____.

2. Ice balls are called _____.

3. All moisture that returns to earth is called _____.

4. The layer of atmosphere closest to the earth is called the _____.

5. Cumulonimbus clouds are _____ with moisture.

6. Swirling wisps of high ice crystals are _____ clouds.

7. _____ is formed by the melting and refreezing of ice crystals.

8. _____ is a mixture of fog and smoke.

B. Write the number of the word next to its definition.

1. contrails	_____ completely filled with moisture
2. inhale	_____ energy that comes in rays
3. irritated	_____ falling moisture from the air
4. pollution	_____ up and down direction
5. precipitation	_____ air covering the earth
6. classified	_____ heights
7. atmosphere	_____ exhaust clouds from jet airplanes
8. vertical	_____ to control
9. altitudes	_____ to breathe in
10. saturated	_____ divided into groups with common traits
11. radiation	_____ feeling discomfort
12. regulate	_____ harmful elements released into the atmosphere

Clouds

Sequencing

Number the sentences to show the order of events in the water cycle.

_____ The droplets of water and ice crystals form raindrops.

_____ The heat from the sun warms the earth.

_____ Water changes to vapor as it travels into the troposphere.

_____ The water on the surface of the earth evaporates.

_____ The droplets of water and ice crystals bunch together and form clouds.

_____ The raindrops become heavier and fall to earth.

■ ■

Cause and Effect

Write the number of each cause on the left on the line in front of its effect.

1. solar energy warms surface water ⬩⬩⬩⬩⬩⬩ _____ hailstones get bigger

2. smog forms over cities _____ a contrail forms

3. the sun warms low stratus clouds _____ water evaporates into the air

4. ice balls bounce up and down _____ they turn into rain

5. thunderheads become saturated _____ heavy showers occur

6. ice crystals hit warmer air _____ clouds form

7. water in jet exhaust condenses _____ people's breathing is affected

8. droplets of vapor bunch together _____ fog disappears

Name _____

Clouds

Here are pictures of four types of clouds mentioned in the story. Name and describe each cloud type.

1	2
_____ _____ _____ _____ _____	_____ _____ _____ _____ _____
3	4
_____ _____ _____ _____	_____ _____ _____ _____

A Biography of John Muir

John Muir was born in Dunbar, Scotland, a coastal town on the North Sea. In February 1849, 10-year-old John, a brother, a sister, and his father sailed across the Atlantic Ocean to America. John's father had heard that there was good farmland in the new state of Wisconsin. The Muirs took a riverboat up the Hudson River to Albany, New York. Then they continued west on the Erie Canal boat to Buffalo and went on to Milwaukee through the Great Lakes. Their travels didn't end there. They traveled another 100 miles into the wilderness by horse and wagon.

John Muir, 1838–1914

The Muirs cleared 80 acres near the Fox River and planted corn and wheat. In November, the rest of the Muir family arrived in Wisconsin. John, his brothers, and his sisters plowed, chopped weeds, hoed, and cut crops by hand. John's father was very strict. The children weren't allowed any breaks during the day, and they worked so hard that their health suffered. Even so, John managed to keep track of the many varieties of birds he saw. He studied nearby wildflowers whenever he could. After the land was worn out from the crops that had been planted, the Muirs moved six miles away and started a new farm.

John wanted to read, but his father thought books were worthless. He didn't allow John to stay up late with his books. He told John he had to get up early in the morning if he wanted to read. It was often too cold to read in the early morning, so John worked on inventions in the cellar. One of his inventions was an early-rising machine. This device kept track of the hours, days of the week, and the months. He whittled all the parts from wood. When it was time to get up, a rod tipped the bed upright, and John greeted the day standing up.

In 1860, when he was 22 years old, Muir took his inventions to the fair in Madison, Wisconsin, and won prizes. His exhibit led to a job in a machine shop and classes at the University of Wisconsin. Muir worked on farms in the summer and taught school in the winter so he could attend the University of Wisconsin when he had time. Muir was interested in all kinds of things. His interest in botany motivated a journey to Canada to study the plants that grew there. When Muir returned to the United States, he went to work in a sawmill in Indianapolis, Indiana, where the owners of the mill gave him time to study plants. In his spare time, Muir invented better ways to make wooden tools. One evening at work, a piece of metal flew into his eye. He couldn't see out of that eye, and the other eye became temporarily blind too.

When his sight returned, John left Indiana and walked 1,000 miles to the Gulf of Mexico, learning about people, nature, and plants. Then he took a boat to California. He arrived in California in 1868 and went to Yosemite Valley. While working as a sheepherder and in a sawmill, John hiked and climbed the mountains, studying glaciers and plants. He began to write about nature for magazines and newspapers.

People all over the world read his stories. Tourists who came to California on the train wanted to see Muir's Yosemite. Many visitors were famous politicians and writers. Muir took President Theodore Roosevelt camping in Yosemite.

In 1889 Robert Underwood Johnson, the editor of *Century* magazine, wanted to see the wildflowers in Yosemite. John explained that sheep had grazed them away. The two men joined forces to save Yosemite. John wrote articles, and Johnson went to Washington, D.C., to convince important people in the government to make Yosemite a national park.

In 1890 Congress passed a law creating Yosemite National Park. The following year President Harrison set aside more land in the western states for national forests. Another president, Theodore Roosevelt, preserved millions of acres in the west for forests and parks.

Muir's writings about plants and nature made people realize it was important to save our forests and areas like Yosemite. His books *The Mountains of California* (1894) and *Our National Parks* (1901) were very popular.

Muir founded the Sierra Club, an organization dedicated to the protection of land, trees, plants, and water. The club is still active today.

John Muir died on December 24, 1914. A stand of giant redwood trees in California was named Muir Woods to honor his work to preserve our natural resources.

Name _____

Questions about *John Muir*

1. List five different kinds of work that John Muir did.

_____

_____

_____

2. How could you tell that learning was of high importance to John?

_____

_____

3. Describe John's early-rising machine.

_____

_____

4. What was Muir's role in saving Yosemite?

_____

_____

_____

5. Do you think Muir was a good writer? Tell why you have that opinion.

_____

_____

6. Do you think it's important to preserve natural areas in our country? Why or why not?

_____

_____

_____

Name _____

John Muir
Vocabulary

A. Write the number of the word next to its definition.

1. varieties   _____   started
2. cellar   _____   the study of plants
3. whittle   _____   many different kinds
4. botany   _____   a slow-moving body of ice
5. exhibit   _____   a group of people who join together; a club
6. temporarily   _____   an underground room
7. glacier   _____   to cut and trim a piece of wood
8. founded   _____   a show or display of objects
9. politicians   _____   for a short period of time
10. organization   _____   a story about a person's life
11. biography   _____   elected officials

B. Circle each adjective below that you think describes John Muir.

lazy   ingenious

studious   hardworking

concerned   adventurous

stingy

C. Find the words in the story to fill in the blanks. The clues will help you decide which words to choose.

1. Parks and national forests help protect our _____

_____.

Clue: Two words that mean land, water, forests, plants, and minerals

2. Muir Woods is a _____ of giant redwood trees.
Clue: A five-letter word that means group or area

3. John Muir worked on his _____ very early in the morning.
Clue: New ideas for doing something

Name _____

John Muir

Make an Information Map

Write at least two facts in each box.

Childhood

Travels

John Muir

Interest in Nature

Writings

Name _____

John Muir

Going Places

A. John Muir hiked and traveled to different places. Fill in the blanks below using the best answers from the places listed in the story. You may need to reread the story to find the answers. For fun, use a globe or a map to trace John Muir's travels.

1. John Muir was born in the country of _____.

2. Dunbar, the town where Muir was born, is located by the _____ Sea.

3. Muir crossed the _____ Ocean to come to America.

4. Muir traveled up the _____ River, along the

   _____ Canal, and across the _____ Lakes to reach his new home.

5. John's family cleared ground for a farm near the Fox River in _____.

6. Muir traveled north to the country of _____ to study plants.

7. Muir walked 1,000 miles to the Gulf of _____.

8. John went to _____ Valley in California.

B. Write names of places in the story that match the following headings. The number after the heading tells how many you should write.

Rivers (2) _____

States (4) _____

_____

Large Bodies of Water (4) _____

_____

Canal (1) _____

Answer Key

Page 6
1. at night
2. The pads help them climb trees.
3. They clean up the earth and keep bacteria and germs from spreading.
4. Their ears turn red, and they stomp their feet, turn to show teeth, scream, click teeth, and give off smelly fluids.
4. Answers will vary. Possible answers are mean, smelly, noisy, bad tempered, hungry.
5. Australia

Page 7
Answers will vary.
1. a. They thought they would harm farm animals. They are noisy, mean, unpleasant animals to have as neighbors.
   b. They realized that they were useful. They clean the earth and keep disease and germs from spreading.
2. They need to eat large amounts of food. If they lived in groups there wouldn't be enough food. They won't eat each other.
3. Tigers, some snakes, etc.
4. Elephants, elk, wolves, whales, chimpanzees, etc.

Page 8
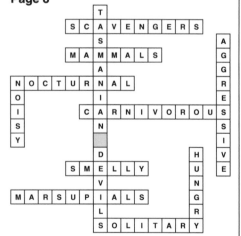

Page 9
Categories—Answers will vary.
Possible answers are:
carnivorous: lions, tigers, dogs
nocturnal: skunks, hippopotamuses, owls
scavenger: hyenas, crows, vultures
marsupial: kangaroos, opossums, koalas

Compound Words
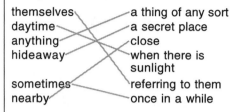

themselves — referring to them
daytime — when there is sunlight
anything — a thing of any sort
hideaway — a secret place
sometimes — once in a while
nearby — close

Page 12
1. Answers will vary; may include the idea of sexual equality; accept any reasonable and defensible response.
2. He was grateful his prayers were answered and people were no longer suffering and ill.
3. On January 1
4. Answers will vary.

5. New Year–d
   Children's Day–i
   Gion Festival–b, f
   Hina Matsuri–c, h
   Boy's Day–a, e
   Tanabata–g

Page 13
1. holiday, festival, celebration
2. emperor, empress, ladies-in-waiting, the minister of state, court musicians, courtiers
3. to a religious shrine
4. sculptures
5. j, c, f, i, g, h, a, d, e, b

Page 14
celebration	celebrate	tion
happiness	happy	ness
beginning	begin	ing
brightly	bright	ly
courageous	courage	ous
collections	collect	tions
valuable	value	able
covered	cover	ed
carefully	care	ful & ly

Sentences will vary.

Page 15
1. strong, courageous fish
2. brightly colored carp kite
3. painted porcelain faces
4. huge decorated boxes
5. bare winter trees
6. enormous ice and snow sculptures

Answers to the bottom section will vary.

Page 18
A. 1. vitamins, minerals
   2. nutritious
   3. calcium
   4. topsoil
   5. tea, dandelion
   6. chickweed
   7. prickly
   8. fires
B. 1. Keep sediment from clogging streams, ponds, and rivers. Provide calcium that is absorbed by algae, which is eaten by fish.
   2. Gardeners have plans for their gardens and don't want weeds popping up where they want flowers or vegetables. Weeds usually die after a few months and look brown and unattractive in the garden.
   3. When the wind blows, it must go around tall weeds. When it does, it deposits soil rather than blowing it away. Weeds hold soil down so it can't be washed or blown away.

Page 19
Answers will vary, but possible answer could include:
1. Weeds are used for food and medicine for people and animals. Weeds provide nutritious vitamins and minerals to plants, animals, and people.
   Weeds provide food for insects.
   Chickweed can be cooked and eaten.
   All the parts of the dandelion can be eaten.
   Dandelions contain vitamins A and C and minerals.
   Bees gather nectar and pollen from weed flowers.
   Weeds provide plants, animals, fish, and people with calcium.
   Decaying weeds add minerals and vitamins to the soil.
   Weeds absorb calcium that is needed by people and animals.
   Calcium is passed along in the food chain from weeds, to animals, to algae, to fish, to people.
   Prickly weeds provide shelter and protection from predators for small animals.
   Weeds are soil builders.
   Weeds hold soil in place, keeping the waterways clean for fish and animals.

Weeds hold soil in place and prevent floods by keeping sediment from blocking streams. Weeds loosen the soil for burrowing animals and other plants.

The wind slows to go around giant weeds, and it leaves some of the soil it is carrying near the weeds.

2. Answers will vary, but might include opinions such as:
Too many weeds will crowd out flowers and vegetables so they can't grow.
Weeds grow very fast. If the weeds aren't pulled out of the garden, there will be more weeds than flowers. If the roots of weeds take all the vitamins and minerals from the soil, there won't be enough nutrients left for the flowers and vegetables.
Weeds look ugly in the garden.
A garden looks well-planned and organized when weeds aren't growing everywhere.

Page 20
A. 10, 6, 5, 8, 4, 9, 2, 7, 1, 3
B. Sentences will vary.

Page 21
decay rot S
predator prey A
absorb soak up S
healthy nutritious S
uninvited welcome A
valuable worthless A
stream river S
soil earth S
benefit harm A
shelter protect S
destroy ruin S
prickly smooth A

Answers will vary, but may include:
1. rested/refreshed/energetic, exhausted/tired
2. silence/quiet, noise
3. stay/remain, relocate/move
4. same, different

Page 24
1. One possible answer is that the teacher recognized her talent and wanted her to have the opportunity for fame and recognition.
2. The school did not accept African-American students.
3. Hotels, trains, and restaurants were segregated so she couldn't

always stay and eat near the places where she sang.
4. to study music and learn languages
5. African Americans were not allowed to perform there.
6. She was the first African American invited to sing a major role there.
7. Answers may vary, but are likely to agree that she was brave because she pursued her dream despite the obstacles of discrimination and segregation.

Page 25
1. Set A: 4, 3, 2, 1
   Set B: 4, 2, 1, 3
   Set C: 3, 1, 4, 2
2. Answers will vary.

Page 26
1. application   7. recognition
2. enroll   8. appointed
3. career   9. segregated
4. foreign   10. discriminated
5. retired   11. competition
6. languages   12. composer

Page 27
1. a. application   b. competition
   c. recognition
2. Answers will vary.
3. a. discriminated   b. segregated
4. a. retirement   b. appointment
   c. enrollment
5. Answers will vary.

Page 30
1. easily shaped; doesn't dissolve in water or body fluids; has a high melting point; reflects sunlight; conducts electricity
2. It costs more to take the gold out than it is worth.
3. *Apollo* spacecraft was coated with gold to protect it from solar heat. Astronauts' faceplates are covered with gold so the sun won't injure their eyes.
4. Answers will vary.
5. South Africa
6. Scoop gravel into a pan. Swirl it and wash with water. Light gravel wahes out and gold stays in the pan.

Page 31
1. Answers will vary. A possible answer: You are worth a great deal because that many pounds (kilograms) of gold have great monetary value.

2. Answers will vary. Possible answer: Something may look like a great opportunity or be very enticing, but looks can be misleading
3. because it is rare
4. Answers will vary. Possible answers are "King Midas and the Golden Touch," "Rumplestiltskin," "The Goose that Laid the Golden Egg," "Jack and the Beanstalk."
Bonus: Student should multiply his or her weight in pounds times 16 and then by $250.

Page 32
A. 1. roll—to press flat
   2. piece—a part of something
   3. see—to use the sense of sight
   4. new—recently made, not used
   5. not—a word used to make a negative statement
   6. karat—a measurement of pureness of gold
   7. so—in order that
B.   Sentences will vary.

Page 33
Students' maps should look like this:

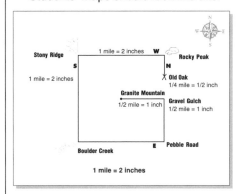

Students should underline "rocky," "stony," "boulder," "pebble," "gravel," and "granite."

Students should circle "pebble" and "gravel."

Page 36
1. They can eat away beams and cause the house to sag or fall.
2. the Amazon Jungle
3. fungi
4. They take them into their houses in the winter; bring them to plants; feed and care for them.
5. The accumulated body heat warms the ants on the inside of the ball. They rotate so no ants get too cold.

6. c, e, b, a, d

Page 37
Synonyms
1. kinds
2. underground
3. dig
4. busy
5. gather
6. enormous
7. build
8. guards

Irregular Plurals
1. fungi
2. larvae
3. leaves
4. cities

Page 38
Pictures may show underground tunnels, mounds, holes in wood or other plant parts, mud packed around a tree branch, or "paper" houses.

Page 39
aphids
bamboo
carpenter
columns
enormous
fungi
grains
harvester
hollow
larvae
mound
saliva
sprout
subterranean
tunnels
weeds

Page 42
1. They had them painted.
2. The person being photographed had to sit without moving for 30 minutes.
3. Answers will vary, but may include ideas such as: They wanted others to see their photos; it was a new, exciting invention and they wanted to be a part of it; having their photos displayed in Brady's studio furthered their fame.
4. He thought it was important to preserve a record of the war for history.
5. They didn't want to be reminded about the war.
6. The government didn't take care of them and money was not given to repair them.
7. His photographs of famous people left a record of what they really looked like. His pictures of the Civil War show us what the war was like.

Page 43
Before:
2. Expose it to iodine vapors.
4. Wait for the plate to turn yellow.
After:
7. Expose the picture to heated mercury.
9. Protect the picture in a glass-covered box.

1830s Daguerreotypes introduced in France.
1844   Brady opened photo studio in New York City.
1851   Brady won a silver medal at the World's Fair in England for his daguerreotypes.
1860   American Civil War began; Brady went to photograph battles.
1871   Congress agreed to buy 2,000 of Brady's war photographs.
1881   Brady closed his studio in Washington, D.C.

Page 44
A. 1. vapors
2. portrait
3. priceless
4. accurate
5. adjustments
6. engravings
7. daguerreotypes
8. retreat

9. studio
10. gallery

B. 1. damage
2. advance
3. popular
4. bright
5. sell
6. won
7. excellent
8. started
9. few

Page 45
A. Proper nouns

Persons	Places
Matthew Brady	France
John Quincy Adams	New York City
William McKinley	England
Abraham Lincoln	Washington, D.C.
King Edward VII	United States
Congress	Canada
	Bull Run

Things
World's Fair
Civil War
Union Army
Battle of Bull Run

B. Common nouns

Persons	Places
artists	army camps
people	studio(s)
person	darkroom
assistants	gallery
presidents	capital
singers	battlefields
writers	
helpers	
sheriff's deputies	
publishers	
generals	
lawmen	

Things
(There are many possibilities.)
equipment
portraits   mercury
collection   books
government   magazines
history

Page 48
1. 1. collect supplies 2. measure 3. cut 4. measure 6 sections 5. fold 6. punch holes 7. tie together
2. paper, scissors, yardstick, or meterstick, pencil, hole punch, ribbon or yarn
3. Answers will vary.

4. 4, 5, 2, 6, 1, 3

Page 49
Answers will vary.

Page 50
1. Any five of the following words: create, decorate, draw, paint, cut, measure, mark, fold
2. Any three of the following verbs: can decorate, could write, will fold, has moved, would like, can be mailed
3. gently wrap
   carefully fold
   fold evenly
   Sentences will vary; verbs should be underlined.

Page 51
1. memory 3   accordion 4
   narrow 2   create 2
   masterpiece 3   measure 2
   treasure 2   panel 2
   photograph 3   collage 2
   holiday 3   envelope 3
   decorate 3   author 2
   summary 3

2. a. collage   d. masterpiece
   b. panel   e. create
   c. summary

3.

Page 54
1. Accept any facts given in the story.
2. strong hooves, patterned body makes it difficult to see young when in tall grass, good eyesight, watch out for each other
3. They know giraffes can see any predators or problems a mile away.
4. Oxpeckers travel on the back of the giraffe, taking off insects, dry skin, and loose hair. The giraffe provides insects for the oxpecker to eat.
5. The giraffe habitat is decreased

and many giraffes are killed for food, hides, and tail hair.
6. The tourists want to see wild animals. This motivates Africans to protect the animals because tourists spend money, providing jobs for Africans.
7. There are laws to protect them and land has been set aside for giraffe habitat.

Page 55
1. I. B. Other animals know they can spot danger a long way away.
   II. A. Each pattern is different.
       B. Some have close-together, straight-edged spots.
       C. Others have irregular spots.
       D. A few are a single color.
   III. A. Stomachs have four sections.
        B. Food mixed with saliva is swallowed whole.
        C. Brings up lumps of food, chews, and swallows again.
        D. Food is digested in the fourth stomach.
2. I. The giraffe has short hair that always looks clean.

Page 56
1. a. crops   e. ruminant
   b. blood vessels f. habitat
   c. irregular   g. moisture
   d. extraordinary h. graze

2. tourist
3. gallop
4. herder

Page 57
Many possible answers. You may want students to locate a partner's answers in the story to confirm.

Page 60
1. The sister ties a bracelet on her brother's wrist and places a circle of red powder on his forehead. The brother gives the sister presents and makes a pledge to care for her. They eat special treats.
2. It is believed that Lakshmi, the goddess of wealth and beauty, will bring good luck to well-lighted places.
3. to give thanks for the rice harvest and the rains
4. Cattle help the farmers grow and harvest the rice.
5. There are costumed people and

decorated animals. There are decorated camels and horses and elephants with flowers painted on their trunks.
6. A mela is a village fair. People buy, trade, and sell goods. There are shows, dances, and singing around campfires.
7. Indians include animals in their festivities. Animals are honored for their work and given special treats.

Page 61
Answers will vary. Two answers for each holiday are needed.
Brother and Sister Day
sister ties a bracelet on her brother's wrist
sister places a red circle on her brother's forehead
special treats
brother gives sister presents
brother promises to protect sister
Ponggal
celebrate rice harvest
give thanks for rain
clean and paint house
new clothes
paint designs on floor and in front of the house
ponggal is made
offering left for gods to thank them for rain and rice
give money to repair temple
honor cattle - bathed, horns painted, decorated with flowers and feathers, paraded, play music for them, given ponggal
Diwali
honors Lakshmi, the goddess of wealth and beauty
houses cleaned and decorated with lights
lights along streets and buildings
special foods
visitors
Republic Day
a great parade of people and animals
elephants' trunks are painted with flowers
camels and horses groomed
people and animals come from long distances to march in the parade
president and crowds watch the parade

Page 62
A. 1. designs   3. plow
   2. religions   4. preparations

B. 1. rahki   5. popular
2. holy   6. ponggal
3. harvest   8. goddess
4. route

Page 63

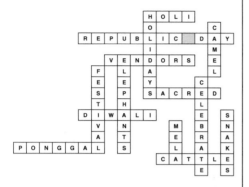

Page 66

1. 1927–Babe Ruth, hit 60
   home runs
   1961–Roger Maris, 61
   1998–Mark McGwire, 70
2. Hank Aaron
3. more people came to games; more
   went to the Baseball Hall of Fame
4. He played in 8 more games.
5. The Yankees had 114 wins in a
   season. The Yankees were 2
   games off the record held by the
   Cubs with 116 wins in 1906.
6. Answers will vary. Baseball is a
   team sport and the outcome of the
   season depends on how well all
   the players play. The total number
   of runs is more important than the
   number of home runs.

Page 67

1. McGwire hugged Sosa. Neither
   boasted that they were better
   than the other. Their statements
   were about how amazing it was
   that they could hit that many
   home runs.
2. Responses will vary.

Page 68

A. 1. greatness of size
2. a lot of excitement
3. a special name people use for
   someone
4. raised
5. one after the other
6. added up
7. unbelievable, amazing
8. theatrical, very impressive

B. batted, blasted, slugged, socked,
slammed, bashed, tally up, sent,
chalked up, added

Page 69

Summaries will vary, but should
include most of the words
in the word box.

Page 72

1. She took an exciting biology class
   and decided that she wanted to
   study that subject.
2. the sea
3. Some insects become immune to
   DDT, causing larger quantities of
   the poison to be used. DDT
   doesn't disappear or decompose
   quickly so DDT is passed along
   the food chain to other animals.
   Animals sicken and often die
   when they absorb DDT. Birds'
   eggs break easily and the young
   are deformed or born dead.
4. If the pesticides were banned, the
   companies that manufactured
   them would lose money and
   possibly go out of business.
5. Scientists researched and
   investigated DDT; Congress
   studied the reports, and laws were
   passed banning the use of DDT in
   the United States.
6. Answers will vary. We might have
   continued to use DDT and harm
   animal life and people.

Page 73

Responses will vary.

Page 74

1. d, e, a, c, b
2. a. money earned for work
   b. a person hired to work
      for another
   c. not for a long time
   d. lasting forever
   e. surroundings
3. temporary, permanent
4. contamination

Page 75

1. the state of being careless
2. to become or make sick
3. in a scientific way
4. full of harm, full of success
5. without harm, without a job
6. having to do with the environs or
   surroundings, having to do with
   those that govern
7. a person who is employed

Page 78

1. paper towel rolls, paper, wrapping
   paper or self-adhesive paper,
   glue, scissors, pen or pencil, ruler,
   other decorations
2. glue
3. Answers will vary.

Page 79

A. 4, 3, 2, 1, 5

B. 1. Decorate the paper if using
   plain paper.
2. Cut a piece of paper 2 1/2" x
   5 1/2" (6.5 x 14 cm)
3. Put glue on the outside of
   the roll.
4. Center the strip of paper around
   the roll.

C. 2, 4, 1, 3, 5

Page 80

Answers will vary.

Page 81

The projects will vary.

Page 84

1. The Aztecs; City of the Gods
2. As tall as a 20-story building;
   500,000 square feet
3. because no one knows who
   built the city or what language
   they spoke
4. The people didn't know how to
   make artifacts from metals. They
   used stone.
5. Opinions will vary.
6. Answers will vary. Possible
   answers: the people were angry at
   the rulers of the city; there was a
   war with other people; there were
   earthquakes or natural disasters

Page 85

A. 9, 3, 7, 10, 8, 5, 4, 1, 6, 2

B. 1. scattered
2. ceramic
3. murals
4. foreigners
5. writing
4. preparations

Page 86

A. 1. a. The mysteries of Teotihuacán
      are unsolved.
    b. It is unclear who the people
      of Teotihuacán were.
   2. unearthed, uncovered
B. 1. discovered
   2. disintegrated

Page 87

Responses will vary.

Page 90

1. all year
2. 5 to 6 months
3. Answers should be yes only if you
are located in a tropical climate.
Students elsewhere should
indicate that the temperatures
where they live are too cold much
of the year.
4. as money
5. sugar, orange water, white rose
powder, cloves, and other spices
6. the top section; the section with
fats, oils, and sweets.

Page 91

A. 1. tropical   6. thrives
   2. pod, trunk 7. pulp
   3. pruned   8. bitter
   4. fertilizer
   5. calories
B. aromatic
C. Answers will vary. Possible
   answers are:
Smell—sweet, aromatic, pleasant
Taste—mouth-watering, sweet,
      delicious
Appearance—deep brown, creamy,
      smooth

Pages 92 and 93

Students are successful if they
follow the directions and play the
game. Answers for matching words
with meanings:
to look over–survey
the part of the plant that holds seeds–
pod
a seed or bean–nib
steps were taken to ready the product
for use–processed
gathered crops–harvested
the energy value of food–calories
order the use of medicine–prescribe
an evergreen tree–cacao
large farm–plantation
circle around the earth that is the
same distance from North and South

Poles–equator
hot and humid climate–tropical
soft, juicy part of a plant–pulp

Page 96

1. Their bodies are heavier and they
have shorter legs.
2. When the eyes blink, they push
against the roof of the mouth and
the food is pushed from the mouth
into the body.
3. It's attached to the front. It can
reach out farther.
4. to lay eggs
5. smooth skin, no poisonous glands,
tubercules on hind feet, stays
underground most of the time
6. The song of the male Fowler's
toad isn't pleasant. The song of the
American toad is melodious. The
American toad has spots on its
chest and belly. The Fowler's toad
does not.

Page 97

1. metamorphosis
2. toxic, toxins
3. estivate
4. a. melodious
   b. external
   c. nocturnal
   d. gelatinlike material
5. having two lives

Page 98

Surinam Toad
habitat: water, tropical
size: 6" (15 cm)
color: brown or gray
legs/feet/body:
   webbed hind feet
   star-shaped tips on front feet
food: small fish, other water animals
eggs: pressed into skin on female's
      back

Bonus:
American Toad
habitat: Eastern U.S. and Canada
size: 1 to 2 inches (2.5–5 cm)
color: brownish olive spots on belly
      and chest
legs/feet/body:
      may list general characteristics
      of all toads
food: beetles, insects, grubs, worms,
      slugs
eggs: hatch after 3 days

Page 99

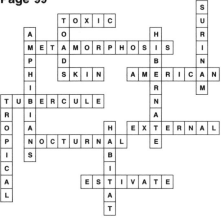

Page 102

1. Tết is celebrated according to the
phases of the moon.
2. to please him so that he will take
good reports about the family to
the Jade Emperor in Heaven
3. They set up an altar and pictures.
They set out food, candles, and
incense. They invite the souls of
their ancestors to share New
Year's Eve dinner. They pray for
their ancestors.
4. a. January, February
   b. 3, 7
   c. kind, arguments
   d. cleaned, decorated, blossoms
5. It's believed that the first visitor
can bring good luck or bad luck.
By choosing the person, they can
be sure that it is a person who will
bring good luck to the household.

Page 103

A. 1. temples, pagodas
   2. incense
   3. ancestors
   4. moon cakes
B. 1. national
   2. lotus
   3. altar
   4. spirits
   5. ceremony
   6. cycle
   7. preserved
   8. Tết
C. Any five of the following:
dumplings filled with pork and
green beans, preserved fruits,
noodles, sweet rice cakes with
beans, fruits, lotus seeds, moon
cakes—a pastry filled with sesame
or bean paste

Page 104

Answers will vary.

I. A. Honored with a special offering to make him happy
   B. At the end of year thought to take reports to the Jade Emperor in Heaven about the family
   C. If the Kitchen God is pleased, the family believes he will praise them

II. A. Pictures are arranged
   B. Food is set out
   C. Candles and incense
   D. Ancestors are invited to share the New Year's Eve dinner

III. A. Buddhists celebrate his birthday every year
   B. Captive birds and fish are set free

IV. A. Children parade with lanterns
   B. Everyone eats moon cakes
   C. Everyone admires the moon

V. A. People go to temples and pagodas
   B. People pray to gods
   C. People pray for their ancestors and a good new year
   D. Children given red envelopes
   E. Family has special treats of lotus seeds and preserved fruit

Page 105

A.

```
M R D V C R M B U J D X E O
P J X I W T B T G T P M Z N
D R G E E A I M U A W B T
X A L T A R N J Q S O L A R
P L A N T I N C E F E E L H
K T U A N C E S T O R S I G
Z L T M G E R S P R I N G T
T E M P L E S Z K T S L H E
S O L G M P W E R U M O T S
T C W E X L R H O N O R S T
P X S Z B J X H K E M L N H
```

B. Sentences will vary.

Page 108

1. He liked the sports and the coach.
2. pentathlon, decathlon
3. He had been paid to play baseball, which was against Olympic rules.
4. Answers will vary.
5. baseball and football
6. Answers will vary, but may include ideas such as:

He was a Native American.
He had many hardships in life.
He was a gifted athlete in many sports.
He had Olympic medals taken away.
He was voted the greatest athlete of the first half of the twentieth century.

Page 109

A. 1. professional
   2. committee
   3. pneumonia
   4. protested
   5. excel
   6. amateur
   7. disqualify
   8. competed
   9. tragedy

B. 1. a
   2. b
   3. c

Page 110

1. reservation
2. education
3. boarding school
4. pentathlon
5. decathlon
6. surpassed
7. major
8. seldom
9. century
10. Olympics

t, t, e, h, a, e, l = athlete

Page 111

1. I. A. Oklahoma
      B. Charlie
      C. farm
      D. athletic games
   II. A. boarding
      B. school
      C. sports
      D. no answer needed
      E. Ran away
2. Answers will vary.
   Possible answers are listed.
      A. Led his teammates to victory in football and track and field
      B. Won the pentathlon and the decathlon in the 1912 Olympic Games
      C. He was an outstanding baseball player
      D. He was an outstanding football player

Page 114

1. warm-blooded vertebrates, two scaly legs, two wings, a beak, feathers, molt, lay eggs
2. An owl can turn its head in a half-circle. The owl's eyes don't move in the eye sockets, so this helps it see things not directly in front of it.
3. The pink coloring in shrimp and algae passes through the flamingo and colors its feathers.
4. empty the water out of its pouch
5. Parrots use their beaks as a third foot to climb trees.
6. ostrich; bigger than a grapefruit

Page 115

1. migrate, talons, captivity, exotic, vertebrates, molt, raptors, sieve
2. a. lakes, rivers
   b. sockets
   c. flock
   d. webbed
   e. backwards, sideways
3. flamingo

Page 116

1. Answers will vary. Possible answer: All birds have characteristics in common.
2. Answers will vary. Possible answer: The different physical characteristics of birds help them adjust to different environments.
3. Answers will vary. Possible answer: In order to survive, birds have learned to eat the food that is available in their habitats.
4. Answers will vary. Possible answers:
   Parrots - can use their beak as a third foot for climbing, strong beak and thick tongue for eating nuts, seeds, fruits
   Pelicans - an expanding pouch on its beak to hold fish
   Flamingos - a beak like a sieve for straining food from mud
   Owls - sharp claws, feathers for silent flight, excellent vision
5. Answers will vary.

Page 117

A. Contractions: don't, here's, won't, it's
   Possessives: world's, bird's, seedeater's, woodpecker's, owl's, flamingo's, macaw's, parrot's

B. 1. boys'
 2. bird's
 3. woman's
 4. horses'
 5. players'
 6. brother's

Page 120
 1. Chile
 2. Answers will vary. Possible answers are south, Andes Mountains, skinny country, Pacific Ocean, Capital–Santiago, vicuña, Strait of Magellan, Antarctica, any of the city names, South America
 3. Answers will vary.
 4. find many different climates and possible activities
 5. the Andes Mountains, the Pacific Ocean

Page 121
 1. d, a, b, c, f, e
 2. swimsuit, sunscreen, northeast, overhead, nearby, horseback, afternoon, breathtaking
 3. soapsuds, moonbeams, bookmark, snowflakes, sunlight, stagecoach, toothpick, folktale
 4. Answers will vary. Example:
 The bar of soap is in the bathtub.
 He poured too much soap, and the suds filled up the sink.
 The soapsuds floated on the water in the bathtub.

Page 122

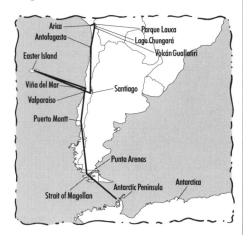

Page 123
 Projects will vary, but should show and tell one or more features of the country.

Page 126
 1. Clouds supply the earth with rain, snow, ice, and storms and regulate solar radiation.
 2. Solar heat causes water on the earth's surface to evaporate and travel into the troposphere. Many tiny drops of vapor gather together to form clouds.
 3. smog, contrails
 4. Clouds are classified by their color, shape, and position in the troposphere (altitude).
 5. thunderhead
 6. rain, snow, sleet, hail

Page 127
 A. 1. evaporate
 2. hail
 3. precipitation
 4. troposphere
 5. saturated (heavy)
 6. cirrus
 7. Sleet
 8. smog
 B. 10, 11, 5, 8, 7, 9, 1, 12, 2, 6, 3, 4

Page 128
 A. 5, 1, 3, 2, 4, 6
 B. 4, 7, 1, 6, 5, 8, 2, 3

Page 129
 1. Cumulus: less than a mile high; woolly-looking shapes; occur on warm, sunny days; can grow and become rain clouds
 2. Cumulonimbus: towering; called thunderheads; as high as 8 miles above earth; saturated with moisture; source of heavy showers, thunder, lightning, tornadoes
 3. Stratus: make the sky look gray, cover the sky, low level, can be on the ground (fog)
 4. Cirrus: high swirling wisps of ice crystals; 5 miles or higher; often have hooks or tufts; called mare's tails

Page 132
 1. Any five of the following: farming, inventing, sheepherding, writing, studying plants, studying nature, sawmill worker, worked in machine shop
 2. He devoted his life and traveled to many places to find out about plants and nature; he was willing to get up early to read or invent things; he worked on inventions even after working all day.
 3. The early-rising machine was carved out of wood. It kept track of the hours, days, and months. When it was time to get up, a rod tipped the bed to an upright position.
 4. The articles John Muir wrote about Yosemite made many people aware of the area and its beauty. Some of those people had power and influence and were instrumental in getting Yosemite designated a national park.
 5. Although answers will vary, students should indicate that he was a good writer because his articles and books were popular and resulted in the creation of parks and national forests.
 6. Answers will vary.

Page 133
 A. 8, 4, 1, 7, 10, 2, 3, 5, 6, 11, 9
 B. These words should be circled: studious, concerned, ingenious, hardworking, adventurous.
 C. 1. natural resources
 2. stand
 3. inventions

Page 134
 Answers will vary.
 Childhood: born in Scotland, father strict, went to America, worked on the farm, liked plants and birds, liked to read, carved inventions from wood

 Travels: went to America, traveled to Wisconsin (boats and wagon), went to Madison, Canada, Indianapolis, hiked to the Gulf of Mexico, California, Yosemite

 Interest in Nature: found time to study birds and plants; went to Canada to study plants; walked 1,000 miles to study plants, people, and nature; studied the mountains and valleys of

California; hiked and climbed the mountains, studying glaciers and plants; founded the Sierra Club

Writings: wrote about nature for magazines and newspapers, wrote two books, *The Mountains of California*, and *Our National Parks*.

Page 135

A. 1. Scotland
   2. North
   3. Atlantic
   4. Hudson, Erie, Great
   5. Wisconsin
   6. Canada
   7. Mexico
   8. Yosemite
B. Rivers: Hudson, Fox
   States: New York, Wisconsin, Indiana, California
   Large Bodies of Water: Atlantic Ocean, Gulf of Mexico, Great Lakes, North Sea
   Canal: Erie